EDITIONS SR

Volume 16

The Promise of Critical Theology

Essays in Honour of
Charles Davis

Marc P. Lalonde, Editor

Published for the Canadian Corporation for Studies in
Religion / Corporation Canadienne des Sciences Religieuses
by Wilfrid Laurier University Press

1995

Canadian Cataloguing in Publication Data

Main entry under title:

The promise of critical theology

(Editions SR ; 16)
Includes bibliographical references and index.
ISBN 0-88920-254-0

1. Davis, Charles, 1923-   2. Theology –
Methodology.   3. Theology, Doctrinal – History –
20th century.   I. Davis, Charles, 1923-
II. Lalonde, Marc P. (Marc Philippe), 1961-
III. Canadian Corporation for Studies in Religion.
IV. Series.

BT78.P76 1995   230'.01   C95-932215-9

BR
118
.P76
1995

Cover design by Leslie Macredie, using a photograph by Claire Davis.
Frontispiece photograph by Michael Manni. Used with permission.

♾

Printed in Canada

The Promise of Critical Theology: Essays in Honour of Charles Davis has been
produced from a manuscript supplied in camera-ready form by the author.

Order from:
WILFRID LAURIER UNIVERSITY PRESS
Waterloo, Ontario, Canada   N2L 3C5

Contents

Rec'd 2/14/96

Acknowledgements

This publication is made possible thanks to the most generous support of Concordia University, Montréal. From the beginning to the end, Concordia's commitment to this project has been unfailing. This support overwhelmingly attests to Concordia's appreciation of Dr. Charles Davis and all he has contributed to the University over the years. In particular, I would like to express my appreciation to the Office of the Dean of Arts and Science; the Office of the Vice-Rector Academic; Internal Grants Services; and the Department of Religion.

I also gratefully acknowledge the participation of those individuals who contributed much to the successful completion of this volume: Florence Henderson-Davis, Michael Oppenheim, Jack Lightstone, David Howes, Abrahim Khan, Mary Eastham, Loretta Gillis, and Bill James. I would also like to thank Linda Chernabrow and Mercy Isaac for their careful preparation of this manuscript throughout its many different phases.

Finally, I would like to express my gratitude to the Canadian Corporation for Studies in Religion; its Publications Officer Martin Rumscheidt; and Wilfrid Laurier University Press for their affirmation and support for this volume in honour of Charles Davis.

Marc P. Lalonde
July 28, 1995
Montréal

Congratulatory Roll

The following individuals wish to express their best wishes to Charles Davis, and to acknowledge, along with the participants in this volume, the achievement and contribution of Charles Davis to Christian theology and religious scholarship.

Gregory Baum, McGill University
Robert McAfee Brown, Pacific School of Religion
Mgr. James F. Coffey, The Parish of Saint Patrick, New York
Rev. John Coventry, S.J., Manresa House, England
Harvey Cox, The Divinity School, Harvard University
Mary Daly, Boston College
Terry Eagleton, Linacre College, Oxford University
Jens Glebe-Moller, University of Copenhagen
Antonio Gaultieri, Carleton University
Jürgen Habermas, University of Frankfurt
Douglas John Hall, McGill University
Adrian Hastings, University of Leeds
Rosemary Haughton, Wellspring House, Gloucester, MA
John Hick, Claremont Graduate School
A. Alistair Kee, The University of Edinburgh
Ursula King, University of Bristol
Hans Küng, Tübingen University
Nicholas Lash, University of Cambridge
Justus George Lawler, Academic Editor, St. Charles, IL
Herbert McCabe, O.P., Blackfriars, Oxford University
S.E. McEvenue, Concordia University
Joseph C. McLelland, McGill University
John C. Meagher, St. Michael's College
J.B. Metz, Münster University
John Milbank, University of Cambridge
Richard Rubenstein, Florida State University
Edward Schillebeeckx, University of Nijmegen

Francis Schüssler Fiorenza, The Divinity School, Harvard University
Rudolf J. Siebert, Western Michigan University
Charles Taylor, McGill University
David Tracy, University of Chicago
Maurice Wiles, Oxford University

Contributors

Daniel Cere completed his PhD with Charles Davis in 1990, and is currently director of Catholic Studies, Newman Centre, McGill University, Montréal.

Charles Davis, one-time professor of Fundamental and Dogmatic Theology at St. Edmund's College, Ware, England, taught in the Department of Religion, Concordia University, Montréal, Québec, from 1970 to 1991. Charles Davis was also Principal of Lonergan University College, Montréal, beginning in 1987. He is now Professor Emeritus at Concordia University, and resides in Cambridge, England, with his family.

Marsha Aileen Hewitt is a former student of Charles Davis, and now teaches at Trinity College, University of Toronto. She is the author of *From Theology to Social Theory: Juan Luis Segundo and the Theology of Liberation* and *Critical Theory of Religion: A Feminist Analysis.*

Paul Lakeland is Professor of Religious Studies at Fairfield University, Fairfield, Connecticut. A former member of the Society of Jesus, Professor Lakeland is the author of two works on political theology, as well as *Theology and Critical Theory: The Discourse of the Church.* He is also co-editor of the new Fortress Press series, Guides to Theological Inquiry.

Marc P. Lalonde is a former student of Charles Davis. He has published articles in *Journal of the American Academy of Religion* and *Studies in Religion/Sciences Religieuses*, among others. He has been undertaking post-doctoral studies at the Catholic University of Leuven, Concordia University, and St. Paul University, Ottawa.

Dennis P. McCann is the author of *Christian Realism and Liberation Theology: Practical Theologies in Creative Conflict* and *New Experiment in Democracy: The Challenge for American Catholicism.* He teaches at De Paul University, Chicago.

Kenneth R. Melchin of St. Paul University, Ottawa, previously studied with Charles Davis in Montréal. He is the author of *History, Ethics and Emergent Probability: Ethics, Society and History in the Work of Bernard Lonergan.*

Michael Oppenheim teaches modern Jewish philosophy at Concordia University, Montréal, and is the author of *What Does Revelation Mean for the Modern Jew? Rosenzweig, Buber, Fackenheim* and *Mutual Upholding: Fashioning Jewish Philosophy through Letters.*

Introduction

Charles Davis and the Promise of Critical Theology

MARC P. LALONDE

I

The essays in this volume have been written for the purpose of honouring one of North America's most impressive religious thinkers, Charles Davis. The occasion is Professor Davis's retirement from active teaching at Concordia University, Montréal, where he served with great distinction for over twenty years.

Prior to coming to North America, Charles Davis was professor of dogmatic theology at St. Edmund's College, Ware, England. It was during this phase of his career that Davis established himself as one of the foremost Roman Catholic theologians in the English-speaking world. Together with contemporaries such as Hans Küng, J.B. Metz, and Gregory Baum, Davis contributed much to the spirit of reform that came to a head during the second Vatican Council. In view of these details, Davis's decision to leave the Roman Catholic Church and its priesthood in 1966 came as a great shock to many, precipitating a fury of public debate and academic discussion.[1] Each of these discourses received a provocative response from Davis in his monumental text *A Question of Conscience*.[2] Here Davis endeavoured to explain and justify his particular course of action at that time: a course which eventually brought him to Canada.

After establishing the Department of Religious Studies at the University of Alberta, Davis accepted an offer to teach at Concordia University in 1970. During his tenure there, Davis produced his most creative and challenging works: *Temptations of Religion* (1973), *Body as Spirit* (1976), *Theology and Political Society* (1980), *What Is Living, What Is Dead in Christianity Today?* (1986), and most recently, *Religion and the Making of Society* (1994).[3] It was also during this period that Davis acted as the Secretary and President

1

of the Canadian Society for Studies in Religion, as well as serving as editor-in-chief of *Studies in Religion/Sciences Religieuses* from 1977 to 1985.

The basic intent of this volume, however, is not so much to relay the facts and details of Charles Davis's life and career. Rather, its principal task is to explore his conceptualization of *critical theology*. While Davis's work in this field of study has certainly made itself felt,[4] it is the conviction of the authors of this text that the profundity and acumen of Davis's contribution demands a more extensive analysis and application. The *telos* which therefore directs the essays assembled here is the perceived need to further scrutinize Davis's version of critical theology and, in so doing, illuminate its promise and the promise of critical religious thought as a whole.

Toward that end, this introduction begins by formulating a basic understanding and characterization of critical theology as evinced in the work of Charles Davis and others. What this explication ultimately discloses is a foundational dilemma that seriously challenges the validity of critical theology itself. It is in light of this problematic that the value of Davis's contribution comes to the fore. The third section of this introduction is thus devoted to elucidating the fundamentals of Davis's critical theology. Finally, I conclude with some prefatory remarks about the individual essays which constitute *The Promise of Critical Theology: Essays in Honour of Charles Davis*.

II

"Critical theology" is a term which designates those theologies in constructive dialogue with the Marxist tradition of social criticism in general, and with the critical theory of the Frankfurt School (i.e., the work of Max Horkheimer, Theodor Adorno, and Herbert Marcuse) and Jürgen Habermas in particular.[5] It is the theological appropriation of this body of literature which initially establishes the uniqueness of critical theology within the recent history of modern Christian thought.[6] What this appropriation presages is an enquiry into the pathologies that mark the development of modernity and religion in relation to the collective and individual emancipation of human beings. Critical theology therefore commences by acknowledging a "dialectic of Enlightenment" as well as a "dialectic of faith."[7] That is to say, critical theology as a theology which intends to augment contemporary human freedom must deal with the serious historical, practical, and conceptual distortions evinced by the project of Enlightenment and the tradition of faith. While both Enlightenment and religion seem to include an interest in emancipation, each tradition has also generated its fair share of human oppression. The critical approach contends that this oppression is not necessarily resolved by a further application of the constitutive principles that figure Enlightened and religious thought. Consequently, the value of these principles are thrown into radical doubt, and the task of the critical thinker is to assess which ones are to be discarded and which ones are to be reconstructed.

So initially we can affirm with Dermot Lane that critical theology "is concerned about putting its own house in order by examining the underlying presuppositions of theology and submitting these to ideology-critique . . . "[8] In other words, critical theology does not presume the validity nor integrity of religious faith, tradition, and praxis merely because they are religious. As finite human creations, they can and have been used to mystify the real sources of human suffering and must be exposed as such. Few religious thinkers have expressed this facet of critical theology as clearly or as forcefully as Charles Davis: "Critical theology acknowledges that the Christian tradition, like other traditions, is not exclusively a source of truth and value, but a vehicle of untruth and false values, and thus must be subject to a critique of ideology and critically appropriated, not simply made one's own in an assimilative process of interpretation."[9]

What Davis is prescribing here is, of course, highly demanding of the theologian and religious adherent alike. However, a self-aware appropriation of religious tradition is essential for any theology that strives to redress the pathologies of modernity and to make critical claims upon a secular pluralist society. Within such a complex and differentiated socio-cultural context, religious ideas cannot be advanced as if they were ready-made metaphysical facts with certain universal application. Instead, all religious claims to truth, normative validity, and sincerity[10] must be publicly justified via an equitable process of open argumentation. Short of this approach, the alternatives commend instrumental strategies that champion the virtues of success rather than mutual respect and understanding. As Jürgen Habermas contends, "the practice of argumentation as a court of appeal . . . makes it possible to continue communicative action with other means when disagreements can no longer be repaired with everyday routines and yet are not to be settled by the direct or strategic use of force."[11] In effect, the critical import and constructive value of religious themes, symbols, narratives, practices, institutions, etc., can only be legitimately secured by openly engaging the claims of other proposals circulating within the contemporary milieu. And as Davis infers, "That indeed implies that moral and religious assertions are always open to counter arguments and revisions."[12]

The core significance and true depth of challenge conveyed by this stipulation for argumentation is clarified in relation to the postmetaphysical conditions of contemporary thought. Following again the work of Habermas, postmetaphysical thinking emerges from various modern developments in social structure, cultural expression, and the accumulation of knowledge which compel the differentiation of metaphysical "Reason" into distinct rationality complexes. Whereas metaphysical reason is rooted in a philosophy of origins (*Ursprungsphilosophie*) that explains the whole of reality by tracing everything back to the "One,"[13] postmetaphysical reason is parcelled out as "three moments—modern science, positive law and post-traditional ethics, and autonomous art and art criticism—but philosophy had precious little to do with this disjunction."[14] In other words, postmeta-physical thinking is oriented by a new non-philosophical or, more to the point, non-idealist model of reason. This model instantiates what Habermas calls a "weak" concept of theory based on empirical investigation, the intersubjective validation of objective facts, and insights gathered and interrelated from all the assorted logics which comprise the store of modern knowledge.[15] In contrast, metaphysical thinking is tied to a "strong" concept of theory. Here "True knowledge relates to what is purely universal, immutable, and necessary. It does not matter whether this is conceived according to the mathematical model as intuition or anamnesis or according to the logical model of thoughtfulness and discourse—the structures of beings are what is laid hold of in knowledge."[16] However, this "laying hold of," says Habermas, falls far below the bar of coherent argument and cogent evidence. It rather represents a purely contemplative claim which harkens back to its mythological point of departure: namely, sacred stories which narrate the *beginnings* of Being and Time.[17] Yet, whether embodied as mythology or metaphysics, the decisive point is that such

> totalizing thinking that aims at the one and the whole was rendered dubious by a *new type of procedural rationality*, which has asserted itself since the seventeenth century through formalism in moral and

legal theory as well as in the institutions of the constitutional state. The philosophy of nature and theories of natural law were confronted with a new species of requirements for justification. These requirements shattered *the cognitive privilege of philosophy.*[18]

In this passage we come upon the crucial insight which recapitulates the critical import of postmetaphysical thinking: the negation of cognitive privilege. What metaphysics holds to, and what the "new species of requirements for justification" cannot abide, is a privileged or precritical explanation of finite existence which entails the suspension of ordinary interaction between self and world in order to explain that interaction in relation to a reality which stands over and above the finite as its ultimate ground and meaning.[19] Armed with the certitude that this foundation is substantiated by the "purely universal, immutable, and necessary,"[20] metaphysical thought is structurally closed to counter argument and revision. Such closure is by no means inconsequential. In principle it implies opposition to the kind of society that tries to solve its problems and bridge its differences via the practice of open argumentation. By implication, to maintain modes of thought that remain rooted in cognitive privilege and its strong concept of theory is to lend support to "the direct or strategic use of force"[21] as an appropriate way to address social disagreement. Against this oppressive alternative, then, a critical postmetaphysical thinking strives to lay bare and eschew any position whose final justification eludes argumentation and radical questioning by taking refuge in an unassailable foundationalism. It is for this reason that Dennis McCann and Charles Strain contend that critical theology "has a promising future only if it avoids any pretence of historical uniqueness, exclusive moral validity, and religious absoluteness. By renouncing these distortions," say the authors, critical theology "will assure a proper place for religious vision in the larger world of public discourse."[22]

However, it is not entirely clear to all students of critical theology exactly where the "distortions" lie, on the one hand; nor is it completely certain that theological thought can truly evade the claim to "religious absoluteness," on the other.

For example, Randy Maddox has complained that "this critical reflection has gone so far as to call into question all classical expressions of Christian tradition as fundamentally distorted."[23] Hardly representing a mere conservative reaction to the subversive character of critical thinking,

Maddox's comment underscores an issue which no "Christian" thinker can ignore. Namely, "For Christian theology, the definitive criterion of truth lies in the revelation of Jesus Christ. This revelation is not just a future ideal, but has taken historical expression. Thus any attempt to formulate a critical theory for reconstructing Christian tradition," he argues, "must find some way of grounding this theory in the historical revelation of Jesus Christ."[24]

According to Douglas Sturm, though, it is precisely this unique "grounding" which eclipses the attempt to "assure a proper place for religious vision in the larger world of public discourse."[25] Sturm calls critical theology to task for its overreliance on technical theological issues (e.g., ecclesiology, christology, and eschatology), and for employing a too-esoteric language in general. "There is, to be sure," Sturm concedes, "nothing intrinsically wrong with these characteristics, but they have the unfortunate result of obscuring one of the basic intentions of . . . [critical] theology, namely, to present an understanding of the world that is of public significance."[26]

To summarize, it seems that Maddox censures critical "theology" for unnecessarily—indeed, wrongly—substituting a criterion of truth extraneous to the revealed truth of God Incarnate. Or to put it in postmetaphysical terms, Maddox emphasizes that the Christian truth as historically revealed by the one and only true God represents the definitive cognitive privilege. To dismiss this privilege as if it were detrimental to the tradition of faith is to dismiss the tradition itself. For his part, Sturm suggests that "critical" theology is not quite critical enough, for it fails to achieve an authentic public discussion which coherently addresses participants who are neither Christian nor religious. He therefore submits that outside of the circle and community of faith, critical theology can have no sustained effect.

What this juxtaposition of views insinuates is that the effort to construct a comprehensive critical theology which neither contradicts the logic of its critical theory nor negates its theological content remains a highly tenuous enterprise. This tenuity reaches us in the form of a dilemma. Can critical theology *as theology* secure its critical operation without forsaking the *logos* of the *theos*?[27]   Similarly, can critical theology *as critical* sustain and cultivate its theological content without renouncing its reliance on critical theory?[28] Otherwise put, is "critical theology" simply an oxymoron when viewed from both sides of its equation?

This particular problematic has not gone unnoticed within extant reviews of the material in question. Dennis McCann's study of *Christian*

Realism and Liberation Theology,[29] for instance, deals with it as a basic contradiction between the method and content of liberation theology. In reference to Gustavo Gutierrez's influential work *A Theology of Liberation,*[30] McCann argues that its bid to logically correlate the Marxist dialectical view of history with an orthodox Catholic reading of the Incarnation ultimately comes to naught.[31] While liberation theology emphatically advances a dialectical vision which "pictures the whole of history as a struggle for liberation,"[32] its theological thematization as "Christ the Liberator"[33] simply does not lend itself to such a framework.[34] "No dialectical *tour de force*" writes McCann, "can integrate the epiphany of the Absolute in time with the vision of history as an ongoing struggle of the oppressed. . . . This is so because the Incarnation makes God the primary agent or 'Subject' in human history, while the dialectical vision makes 'it possible for men to enter the historical process as responsible subjects.' "[35] Thus, if it is necessary—as Maddox would have it—that " any attempt to formulate a critical theory for reconstructing Christian tradition must find some way of grounding this theory in the historical revelation of Jesus Christ,"[36] then McCann's analysis suggests that this condition remains insufficient by itself.

Given this impasse, it may prove helpful to examine a more complex methodological and systematic appropriation of critical theory. Here we need look no further than Helmut Peukert's important treatise, *Science, Action, and Fundamental Theology: Toward a Theology of Communicative Action.*[37] In this work, Peukert argues that the theory of communicative action as developed by Habermas demands a theological foundation if this theory is to maintain its rational coherency and critical rigour. In this way, Peukert extends the validity and legitimacy of contemporary models of scientific rationality to the discipline of theology. He thus attempts to establish two main points. As the author has expressed it elsewhere:

> Both projects, theology as well as Enlightenment, need to enter into public conversation with each other to continue. This is clear for the project of theology insofar as it makes a claim to speak in a way that is understandable and reasonable to all. And, to my mind, this claim constitutively belongs to theology which then, however, must become engaged in the argumentative discourse. But my thesis is that the Enlightenment also handicaps itself if it does not face the challenge of the religious traditions of humanity and their reflective formulations in

theologies in which the basic human condition has been reflected upon in a radical way.[38]

In effect, Peukert aspires to demonstrate via a process of open argumentation how theology can justify itself as critical and, in doing so, maintain itself as preeminently "theo-logical." Though it is beyond the scope of this introduction to give a detailed exposition and critique of Peukert's complicated proposal,[39] it is possible to indicate its principle line of argument so as to clarify exactly what is at stake in "the promise of critical theology."

Peukert commences his argument by suggesting that "The convincing claim of scientific critique led to the fact that its standard did not remain external to theology itself but, by way of historical-critical inquiry, has even carried the day in theology itself. Modern theology is unthinkable without this solidarity in critique."[40] In keeping with this insight, Peukert undertakes an extensive dialogue with the most recent theories of science "in order to develop a proposal for a 'fundamental theology,' that is, a kind of foundational theory of theology. It is in my view" continues Peukert, "that a certain convergence can be established between contemporary reflection on the fundamental principles of theology on the one side and the results of research into the theory of science on the other. It seems to me that the point of convergence lies in a theory of communicative action."[41]

Communicative action, according to Habermas, is human action mediated by speech acts aimed at reaching mutual understanding and agreement. It serves to establish a nonviolent, noninstrumental procedure for justifying and coordinating interpersonal relations based on rational consensus. This consensus is attained by complying with the implicit universal validity claims of communicative competence. This theory holds that there are three universal validity claims signified within every ordinary speech act: truth, normative rightness, and truthfulness. Each of these is matched with an appropriate mode of argumentation: scientific discourse, practical discourse, and aesthetic discourse respectively.[42] The structure of communicative action and its rationality then, advances an intersubjective paradigm and framework for social critical theory: one which accents the primacy of our interactive partners for the creation of a reflective self-understanding and identity.[43]

The specific "point of convergence" between communicative action and theology that Peukert eventually discloses is actually an *aporia* in the structure of communicative action itself: namely, the death of the innocent other in history. Peukert claims that if the theory of communicative action is to constitute the normative foundation or core for the identity of the human subject interacting in society and history, then this theory must—for the sake of its rational coherence—extend to include those persons whose previous existence contributed to the formation and substance of this identity.[44] In other words, communicative solidarity with the dead is required by the logic of communicative action. If such a solidarity is deemed impossible, then the identity formed in the crucible of communicative action would prove to be a deception. However, rather than concluding that the theory of communicative action should be abandoned altogether, Peukert seeks to complete it by demonstrating how the praxis of communicative action points beyond itself to a reality that saves the other in death, and therefore, saves the very identity made possible by communicative action. As Peukert expresses the matter:

> This reality disclosed in communicative action, asserted as the saving reality for others and at the same time as the reality that through this salvation of the other makes possible one's own temporal existence unto death, must be called "*God*." Within a situation of communicative action, . . . the reality of God becomes *identifiable* and *nameable* through the communicative action itself. In this way, the basic situation of the disclosure of the reality of God and its identifiability, and hence at the same time the origin of possible discourse about God, are given.[45]

The "identity" and "name" of God which Peukert ultimately professes is the risen Christ: "The resurrection of Jesus" says Peukert, "can be understood as the empowerment to live such an existence [i.e., anamnestic existence in universal solidarity] and to witness it for others—that is, to manifest the possibility of such an existence though the manner of one's own communicative action."[46] It is in this fashion that Peukert illustrates how communicative action is "the central thesis of the whole of theology"[47] and *mutatis mutandis*, how theology is the "central thesis" of the whole of communicative action.

How convincing is this argument?

Well, according to both Thomas McCarthy and Dennis McCann, not very. For his part, McCarthy observes that Peukert's critique of communicative action constitutes a variation on the Kantian postulate argument for moral reason and action. In the postcosmological situation outlined in Kant's critique of pure reason, selfish human beings cannot fulfil the universal moral imperative to pursue the good for all lest they "postulate the existence of an infinite moral being who has the power to produce the necessary harmony between"[48] the imperative and human nature. In an analogous fashion, Peukert advances a thesis which proffers that the universal solidarity required by a theory of communicative action is thought to disintegrate lest it postulate the resurrection of Jesus Christ. It is for this reason that McCann has charged that Peukert's hypothesis constitutes a typical apologetic ploy that ultimately brackets Christian theology from a full-fledged, self-critical appraisal. As McCann points out, "Any theological conversation with [Habermas] . . . must begin with a willingness to be equally honest in discussing the claims of one's own religious tradition. It cannot proceed on a business-as-usual basis, as if a raid on the Frankfurt School could be carried off as one more successful exercise in 'spoiling the Egyptians.' . . . Instead of engaging in rigorous criticism of theology's foundations, for the most part . . . [Peukert has] staged thematic confrontations designed to provide an opening for more kerygmatic preaching."[49] It therefore comes as no surprise that Peukert is able to discover the resurrected Christ at the centre of the reality disclosed within communicative action. Or as McCarthy puts it: "Religious *experience* and religious *tradition* remain key ingredients in [Peukert's] account of faith, which is thus not presented as susceptible of purely argumentative reconstruction."[50]

In spite of the general veracity of McCarthy's statement, its diagnosis here is too imprecise. For how in the world can one produce an account of faith without referring to religious experience and tradition? Would it be at all reasonable, say, to demand from McCarthy an account of critical reason which forgoes all reference to the Enlightenment tradition or the unique historical experiences that have shaped the character of critical theory?[51] The main difficulty with Peukert's proposal is not its focus upon religious experience and tradition per se, but its implicit utilization of their doctrinal formulation. What this utilization both permits and entails is an account of faith as the saving knowledge; as the one and only cognitive privilege capable of mending the *aporia* spied in the theory of communicative action. To contend that this theory fails because it cannot guarantee its results is merely another way of saying that it lacks a strong concept of theory. It is this concept which Peukert's fundamental theology provides Habermas's theory of communicative action. Consequently, Peukert must, as a matter of course, evade "rigorous criticism of theology's foundations."[52] Only in this way can the cognitive privilege at work in Peukert's theology remain unscathed by its encounter with Habermas's critical theory.

In view of the preceding discussion and the review of Peukert's work, we are bound to ask whether "critical theology" is possible. Can contemporary religious thought elude the need for a cognitive privilege? Is such a privilege simply the *sine qua non* of all authentic theological thought? If not, what religious idea can serve as its basis for reconstruction?

It is perhaps due to these and other difficulties encountered in the project of critical theology that Davis stresses "how much is still to be done before one can speak of a critical theology in more than a pretentious way."[53] Yet in spite of this admission, the present volume holds that Davis's own contribution dispels a good measure of this "pretension," providing much-needed insight into the cultivation of a progressive religious thinking. It is to the details of this contribution, then, that we now turn.

III

"As used here the word [critical] does indeed mean" writes Davis, "that any worthwhile theology should question its assumptions and not be the parroting of an unexamined tradition. It implies, too, that reason in theology as elsewhere is critical as having a negative function in dissolving habitual and inadequate modes of thought and action."[54]

With this succinct characterization of critical reason set loose on theology, we are immediately introduced to the most conspicuous feature of Davis's work: *the critique of religious orthodoxy*. As Davis interprets it, religious orthodoxy constitutes the preeminent expression of "an unexamined tradition," and one of his fundamental goals is to unmask it as a "habitual and inadequate mode of thought and action." From *A Question of Conscience* through to *Religion and the Making of Society*, Davis charts the end of orthodoxy as the logical repercussion of a genuine critical theology.[55] In this way, he achieves exactly what McCann accused Peukert of evading, namely, a rigorous critique of the foundations of theological thought.

However, Davis's proposal is far more involved than this negative conclusion suggests by itself. To begin with, one of its central claims concerns the contiguity of faith and radical criticism. The value of Davis's critical theology as both critical and theological hinges upon the assertion that faith entails an authentic critical moment. To be sure, this moment significantly alters what counts as theological content as Davis's critique of religious orthodoxy will illustrate. Nevertheless, the point is that the theological application of critical reason does not represent the mere imposition of an extraneous criterion of truth but is a piece with faith working on itself as faith.

With this hypothesis in view, we are in a better position to see that the critique of religious orthodoxy serves more than example. Indeed, what it intends to establish is the critical authenticity of faith as the critique of cognitive privilege. In contrast to the orthodox interpretation, Davis contends that faith resists and ultimately negates its reduction to a form of knowledge. As such, it must be understood as otherwise than metaphysics; as otherwise than a strong concept of theory; as otherwise than a "True knowledge [that] relates to what is purely universal, immutable, and necessary."[56]

However, Davis's explication of faith reveals more than a postmetaphysical supposition. This is to say, that faith's critique of cognitive privilege cannot be solely accounted for by the differentiation of metaphysical "Reason" into distinct rationality complexes however compatible such a development may be. Rather, it emerges from an action and praxis which elicits the transformation of self and world as opposed to their theoretical reconstitution.

Davis's version of critical theology commences by arguing that the primacy of praxis advocated by critical theory is incompatible with any notion of religious orthodoxy. Such primacy implies that cultural phenomena—of whatever kind—are the products of human action and inevitably share the limitations and deformations which attend all finite forms of social intercourse. Religious orthodoxy, however, conceives doctrine as an absolute norm which confers primacy to theory.[57] As Davis elaborates:

> Religion when maintained as an orthodoxy claims a permanent self-identity, remaining unscathed by social and practical changes. It invokes some purely theoretical centre of reference to serve in an abstract way as a norm of identity. There are indeed conflicting orthodoxies, but the differences are conceived as basically theoretical.

> The presupposition of orthodoxy is the contemplative conception of
> knowledge, according to which knowledge is the result of the
> disinterested viewing of reality by individuals. Orthodoxy is that
> contemplative conception applied to religious truth.[58]

Orthodoxy presumes that knowledge is foundational for religious faith.
To possess this knowledge—in this case, knowledge of God and salvation—is
to control the key which unlocks the truth and meaning of reality in its
totality. Historical and social change are therefore witnessed as corresponding
to or deviating from an ontological constant. Whether one is examining the
dialectic of enlightenment or the theory of communicative action, its value
and meaning is discerned in relation to, or bent to conform with, the
theoretical structure implicit to orthodoxy which cannot relinquish its total
grasp of the situation without forsaking itself. Religious orthodoxy, so
understood, comprises a form of identity thinking: it labours to subdue
difference, contradiction, and anomaly.

Davis further explains the development of religious orthodoxy as an
effort to conceptualize the mythic or narrative configuration which shapes the
initial expression of the Christian faith. In its early formation, the Christian
tradition functions as a cosmology which provides "a comprehensive account
of the order of the world, of society and nature and the destiny of the
individual."[59] As a total world view, its portrayal of reality is implicity
accepted as unalterable, thus furnishing a fundamental backdrop for the
propagation of knowledge, communication, and interaction. For its part,
orthodoxy draws upon the form of human intelligence at work within this
paradigm. It is apprehended as *"faith seeking understanding,"* that is, "as the
analysis, formulation, and defense of elements of myth as doctrines. Thus the
mythical mode of interpretation of Christianity corresponds to the doctrinal
or dogmatic mode of interpretation."[60]

This doctrinal exegesis obtains its ideal idiom as an "ontotheology." As
Davis clarifies, "Ontotheology is the attempt to translate the content of the
Christian myth into the theoretical concepts and statements of metaphysical
philosophy."[61] The problem with this translation, however, is its bid to
claim the certitude appropriate to myth (i.e., the trust which emerges when
narrative comprises the integral framework for practical experience) for a
genre which, in principle, does not allow for such an existential conviction.
This is to say, that theoretical knowledge is, of its very nature, provisional
and limited.[62] In reference to Habermas's critical theory, Davis writes that

"as soon as one clearly distinguishes the cognitive from the normative and expressive, one has to recognize that human knowledge is limited and fragmentary, changing and relative. Comprehensive explanations remain largely hypothetical."[63] In view of this diagnosis, both ontotheology and orthodoxy are remnants of a superseded plausibility structure. The effort to maintain that structure in the face of its demise represents a "lust for certitude"[64] rather than an attempt to nourish the faith. Indeed, the misappropriation of narrative certitude displaces the experiential basis for its surety with the pseudo-certitude of dogma which frustrates the dynamic practice of faith.[65] Thus, "in religion direct attempts to achieve certitude are self-defeating. Each system of faith . . . become[s] closed in on itself by efforts to keep its adherents in absolute certitude. Such self-enclosure violates the nature of religious faith, which implies a self-transcending openness to total reality."[66]

As the above analysis suggests, Davis holds that there is a certitude appropriate to faith. However, in direct contrast to orthodoxy and ontotheology, this certitude remains "unsought,"[67] the blessing of a free gift of love rather than the assurance of a forced conclusion. Davis writes:

> The absoluteness of faith is the absoluteness of total demand and total response in an experience of unrestricted love in relation to hidden transcendence or mystery. Faith is the drive toward transcendence, the thrust of human beings out of and beyond themselves, out of and beyond all the limited orders and human certainties under which they live, in an attempt to open themselves to the totality of existence and reach unlimited reality and ultimate value. It is a total response to the felt reality of a total demand. That absoluteness should not be confused with a certitude of beliefs.[68]

In many ways, this passage unveils the crux of Davis's position: namely, the fundamental distinction between faith and belief. Religious belief systems, like human knowledge in general, "are the changing limited culturally particular manifestation of religious faith."[69] As such, they are, in principle, always subject to error and in need of constant criticism.[70] Faith, on the other hand, is absolute transcendence and represents a complete, utterly self-effacing openness to Reality as Unlimited and Infinite. "As an orientation," asserts Davis, "it has a term, 'The Transcendent,' but no object, because the Transcendent remains unknown. The term of the response of faith is mystery, because we have no proper knowledge of the Transcendent. We cannot," he continues, "grasp the Transcendent as an object; we can merely indicate the Infinite, the Unlimited, through symbols."[71] In short, faith for Davis is mystical, not mythical. And as mystical, it tends to nullify any particular claim to religious knowledge which declares more than is warranted by an ineffable experience of the divine.[72]

It is at this juncture where the contiguity of faith and radical criticism announces itself most clearly. Understood as complete transcendence, faith entails the negation of all positive identifications of the Absolute. In this way, it lends itself to a form of nonidentity thinking, that is, to a type of critical thinking which punctuates the contradictions that exist between the concept and the reality or object it claims to represent.[73] It is in view of this point of contact that Davis claims, for instance, that both faith and critical reason "are in principle opposed to orthodoxy, each demanding in its own way that one see for oneself."[74]

What Davis ultimately sees here is a constructive role for religious faith in the postmetaphysical situation. He contends that faith's transcendence can serve to keep the argument open, resisting any finite explication of human existence as complete or final in itself.[75] Yet over and above the postmetaphysical differentiation of metaphysical "Reason" into distinct rationality complexes, faith injects the difference of an otherness which repels all temptations to ontological reduction. This is to say, that beyond the procedural disintegration of a totalizing thinking, faith as the very *"drive toward transcendence"*[76] constitutes the non-totalizing totality that limits even the most modest of claims. In this way, faith prevents human reason from abandoning its critical function; from identifying itself with the Absolute; from closing in on itself as the immanent explanation of the whole of reality; from becoming the mere tool of the controlling Subject. As Davis reminds us: "Human rationality, when taken beyond the efficient adaptation of means to ends, is a more fragile and elusive achievement than we often realize. Paradoxically, it requires religious faith for its survival."[77]

The above exposition is perhaps a more involved way of stating that "Christian faith is a transformative principle, not a body of objective knowledge."[78] As such, it tends to resist the imposition of a cognitive privilege as that which obstructs and obscures faith's transforming dynamic. Yet as transforming, it lends itself immediately to praxis. "Quite aside from any reference to the Marxist view of the primacy of practice," writes Davis, "there is a particular, religious reason for refusing to give Christian religion a theoretical centre of reference . . . it is that Christian practice is a response to the reality of a transcendent gift; it is the living out of the concrete experience of transcendent reality."[79] It is for this reason that Davis urges a pragmatic conception of the Christian tradition as a whole.[80] As he emphatically states the matter: "The message of revelation is a *praxis*, an ethical life, a way of being and acting. It may be partially articulated in propositions. It may stimulate theoretical reflection. But it is essentially the establishment of a practical way of life."[81]

What are the theological ramifications of such an establishment?

For one thing, this pragmatic vision of religious tradition does not—indeed cannot—abandon the critical moment of faith. This is evinced by the fact that both faith and the primacy of praxis stand in critical opposition to religious orthodoxy and the primacy of theory. The theology of a trans-formative faith is necessarily a critical theology; is necessarily a mode of religious thinking that strives to further the transformation of self and world. To be sure, such a theology "cannot proceed on a business-as-usual basis"[82] as McCann pointed out. For his part, Davis makes clear its subversive, revolutionary effect:

> if the mediation of faith through *praxis* is consistently accepted, that means the destruction of theology in the current sense of the articulation of the immanent self-understanding of faith. Theology loses its boundaries as an independent discipline, because the only appropriate context for the conscious articulation of *praxis* is a theory of the development of society in its total reality.[83]

Thus, the promise of critical theology is the negation of those types of theology and religious discourse which ultimately frustrate the transformative principle of faith. The goal here is not to create more elaborate systematic theologies, but to recreate society in view of the experience of a transformative faith. In effect, the promise of critical theology as such is inextricably bound to the promise of faith. What, then, is its promise? What particular religious ideas, themes, symbols, stories, etc., seem appropriate or even vital for its concrete expression? What is to be the self-understanding of the religious thinker who is preoccupied herself or himself with such a task? How should the community of faith receive its transformative message, and what are the implications for the structure and meaning of that community? What other sources aside from critical theory might aid the transformative promise of faith? What might be the contribution of other religious traditions and philosophies? Of other critical perspectives rooted in very particular social, cultural, and historical experiences?

IV

It is in response to these and other questions that the authors of this volume endeavour to reflect and build upon the promise of critical theology.

Leading the way is a programmatic reflection by Charles Davis himself on "Theology for Tomorrow." In this piece, Davis reviews the basis and direction of his own work to date while speculating upon its future orientation. Taking up the challenge of certain postmodern issues and concerns, Davis introduces the theme of the religious supernatural as an idea which could very well represent an essential addition to a future critical theology.

In "For Whom Do We Write? The Responsibility of the Theologian," Paul Lakeland addresses the future position, role, and status of the critical theologian working within the Catholic tradition of faith. Considering the life and work of Charles Davis as an important model in this regard, and relying on critical insights expounded by Benjamin, Gramsci, and Said, Lakeland offers an argument on behalf of the secular lay theologian who remains free from the official Church while seriously attending to the needs and concerns of the larger community of faith.

What these needs and concerns should be constitutes a central theme in Dennis P. McCann's essay, "The Path Marked Out by Charles Davis's Critique of Political Theology." By comparing and contrasting Davis's vision of a future Church in *A Question of Conscience* with his critique of theology and society in *Theology and Political Society*, McCann argues that the effort to radically reform the Church represents an essential moment of political responsibility for the Christian committed to the transformative values of faith.

In Kenneth R. Melchin's contribution, "Pluralism, Conflict, and the Structure of the Public Good," the author also pursues a dialogue with Davis's *Theology and Political Society*. In this case, Melchin supplements Davis's social and political concerns with the ideas advanced within the field of conflict studies. What this body of literature provides, Melchin indicates, is practical, concrete insight into the potential formation of emancipatory discourse within a pluralistic society.

That this potential is partially linked to the conceptualization of pluralism itself is the topic of Michael Oppenheim's article, "Welcoming the Other: The Philosophical Foundations for Pluralism in the Works of Charles Davis and Emmanuel Levinas." As might be expected, Oppenheim illustrates that the respective visions of religious pluralism in Davis and Levinas are inherently effected by the different religious traditions which inform their work. After a thorough review of Davis and Levinas on this issue, Oppenheim comes to suggest that while Davis tends to undervalue religious particularism in favour of a religious universalism, Levinas advances the opposite scenario. However, it is not Oppenheim's aim to judge which attitude is the better, but to analyze the various implications that these alternative depictions of pluralism entail for religious discourse.

Very much in keeping with Oppenheim's concern for "welcoming the other" is Marsha A. Hewitt's essay, "Charles Davis and the 'Warm Current' of Critical Theology: A Feminist Critical Appreciation." Picking up on Davis's affirmation of feminist theology in *What Is Living, What Is Dead in Christianity Today?*, Hewitt proceeds to flesh out this declaration by exploring the intersecting points between Davis's critical theology and much of feminist critical theory and religious reflection. In this way, Hewitt intends to contribute to Davis's critical project by illustrating how the feminist approach augments the critical thrust of a socially and politically mediated faith.

The essays in this text, I feel, attest to the depth, profundity, and erudition of Charles Davis's accomplishments. It is the hope of the editor and the individual contributors that this initial examination of Charles Davis's critical theology will encourage others to delve further into its challenge and consequence.

Notes

1   In Richard P. McBrien's book, *Report on the Church: Catholicism After Vatican II* (San Francisco: HarperSanfrancisco, 1992), the author accurately summarizes the significance of Davis's decision when he writes that "Davis's departure from the Church was a turning point in post-conciliar Catholicism. It signalled a new spirit of criticism in the Church, [and] a new sense of impatience with the pace of change" (205).

2   New York: Harper & Row, 1967.

3   For further details on these and other works, see the Selected Bibliography at the end of this volume.

4   See Tom Bottomore, *The Frankfurt School* (London: Tavistock, 1984), 78; Joseph Kroger, "Prophetic-Critical and Practical-Strategic Tasks of Theology," *Theological Studies* 46 (1985): 3-20; Bruce Grelle, "Christian Political Ethics and Western Marxism," *The Journal of Religious Ethics* 15 (Fall 1987): 173-98.

5   For a thorough overview of the history and meaning of critical theory see David Held, *Introduction to Critical Theory: Horkheimer to Habermas* (Berkeley: University of California Press, 1980).

6   Alfredo Fierro, *The Militant Gospel: A Critical Introduction to Political Theologies* (Maryknoll, NY: Orbis Books, 1977), 108.

7   See Max Horkheimer and Theodor W. Adorno, *Dialectic of Enlightenment* (New York: Continuum, 1990), 3-42; and Rudolf Siebert, "From Conservative to Critical Political Theology," in James A. Riemer, ed., *The Influence of the Frankfurt School on Contemporary Theology: Critical Theory and the Future of Religion* (Lewiston, NY: Edwin Mellen Press, 1992), 176.

8   Dermot A. Lane, *Foundations for a Social Theology: Praxis, Process and Salvation* (New York: Paulist Press, 1984), 33.

9   Charles Davis, *Theology and Political Society* (Cambridge: Cambridge University Press, 1980), 25.

10 These terms derive from Jürgen Habermas's theory of communicative competence and action. For further comment on Habermas's work see below in this introduction.

11 Jürgen Habermas, *Reason and the Rationalization of Society*, Vol. 1 of *The Theory of Communicative Action* (Boston: Beacon Press, 1984), 17-18.

12 Davis, *Theology and Political Society*, 178.

13 Jürgen Habermas, *Postmetaphysical Thinking: Philosophical Essays* (Cambridge, MA: MIT Press, 1992), 115.

14 Jürgen Habermas, *Moral Consciousness and Communicative Action* (Cambridge, MA: MIT Press, 1990), 17.

15 Jürgen Habermas, *The Philosophical Discourse of Modernity: Twelve Lectures* (Cambridge, MA: MIT Press, 1987), 408, no. 28.

16 Habermas, *Postmetaphysical Thinking*, 13.

17 Ibid., 31, 118-24.

18 Ibid., 33.

19 Ibid., 32, 51.

20 Ibid., 13.

21 Habermas, *Reason and the Rationalization*, 18.

22 Dennis P. McCann and Charles R. Strain, *Polity and Praxis: A Program for American Practical Theology* (Minneapolis: Winston Press, 1985), 3.

23 Randy L. Maddox, "Contemporary Hermeneutic Philosophy and Theological Studies," *Religious Studies* 21 (1985): 529.

24   Ibid.

25   McCann and Strain, *Polity and Praxis*, 3.

26   Douglas Sturm, "Praxis and Promise: On the Ethics of Political Theology," *Ethics* 92 (July 1982): 737.

27   This question conveys the main point which substantiates Jürgen Habermas's objections to critical theology.   See his essay, "Transcendence from Within, Transcendence in This World," in Don S. Browning and Francis Schüssler Fiorenza, eds., *Habermas, Modernity, and Public Theology* (New York: Crossroad, 1992), 226-50.

28   This question represents the core assertion of John Milbank's book, *Theology and Social Theory: Beyond Secular Reason* (Oxford: Basil Blackwell, 1990). For further insight into Milbank's thesis, see Charles Davis's essay in this volume.

29   Dennis P. McCann, *Christian Realism and Liberation Theology: Practical Theologies in Creative Conflict* (Maryknoll, NY: Orbis Books, 1981).

30   Gustavo Gutierrez, *A Theology of Liberation: History, Politics, and Salvation* (Maryknoll, NY: Orbis Books, 1988).

31   McCann, *Christian Realism and Liberation Theology*, 230.

32   Ibid., 168.

33   Gutierrez, *A Theology of Liberation*, 102-105.

34   McCann, *Christian Realism and Liberation Theology*, 183.

35   Ibid., 184.

36   Maddox, "Contemporary Hermeneutic Philosophy," 529.

37   Cambridge, MA: MIT Press, 1986.

38   Helmut Peukert, "Enlightenment and Theology as Unfinished Projects," in Browning and Fiorenza, eds., *Habermas, Modernity, and Public Theology*, 45.

39   For a more concise version of Peukert's argument see his essay, "Fundamental Theology and Communicative Praxis as the Ethics of Universal Solidarity," in Reimer, ed., *The Influence of the Frankfurt School*, 221-46.

40   Peukert, *Science, Action, and Fundamental Theology*, 155.

41   Ibid., xxiii.

42   See Jürgen Habermas, "What is Universal Pragmatics?" in *Communication and the Evolution of Society* (Boston: Beacon Press, 1979), 1-68.

43   Ibid., 1, 34.

44   Peukert, *Science, Action, and Fundamental Theology*, 171-72.

45   Ibid., 245.

46   Ibid., 226-27.

47   Ibid., 171.

48   Thomas McCarthy, "Critical Theory and Political Theology: The Postulates of Communicative Reason," in *Ideals and Illusions: On Reconstruction and*

Deconstruction in Contemporary Critical Theory (Cambridge, MA: MIT Press, 1991), 204.

49 Dennis P. McCann, "Habermas and the Theologians," *Religious Studies Review* 7 (January 1981): 20.

50 McCarthy, "Critical Theory and Political Theology," 215.

51 See, for example, Helmut Dubiel's study, *Theory and Politics: Studies in the Development in Critical Theory* (Cambridge, MA: MIT Press, 1985).

52 McCann, "Habermas and the Theologians," 20.

53 Charles Davis, *What Is Living, What Is Dead in Christianity Today?* (San Francisco: Harper & Row, 1986), 4.

54 Davis, *Theology and Political Society*, 104.

55 It is for this reason that I have elsewhere depicted Davis's work as a *postorthodox* critical theology. See my essay, "From Postmodernity to Postorthodoxy, Or Charles Davis and the Contemporary Context of Christian Theology," *Studies in Religion/Sciences Religieuses* 22, no.4 (1994): 437-49.

56 Habermas, *Postmetaphysical Thinking*, 13.

57 Davis, *Theology and Political Society*, 2.

58 Ibid., 130.

59 Davis, *What Is Living?*, 25.

60 Ibid., 30.

61 Ibid., 60.

62 Ibid., 109.

63 Charles Davis, *Religion and the Making of Society: Essays in Social Theology* (Cambridge: Cambridge University Press, 1994), 27.

64 Charles Davis, *Temptations of Religion* (New York: Harper & Row, 1973), 1-27.

65 Davis, *What Is Living?*, 71.

66 Davis, *Temptations*, 15.

67 Ibid., 24.

68 Davis, *What Is Living?*, 67.

69 Davis, *Religion and the Making of Society*, 35.

70 Davis, *What Is Living?*, 67.

71 Davis, *Religion and the Making of Society*, 35.

72 Davis, *What Is Living?*, 51.

73 For further insight about non identity thinking see Theodor W. Adorno, *Negative Dialectics* (New York: Seabury Press, 1973).

74 Davis, *What Is Living?*, 53.

75 Davis, *Religion and the Making of Society*, 36-37.

76 Davis, *What Is Living?*, 67. Italics added.

77   Davis, *Religion and the Making of Society*, 37.

78   Davis, *What Is Living?*, 71.

79   Ibid., 78.

80   Ibid., 35-45.

81   Davis, *Religion and the Making of Society*, 99.

82   McCann, "Habermas and the Theologians," 20.

83   Davis, *Religion and the Making of Society*, 91.

One

Theology for Tomorrow

CHARLES DAVIS

I

From time to time I have been led to write programmatic essays on what theology should do and be. The earliest of these essays is "Theology and Its Present Task," written for the Downside Symposium on *Theology and the University*, edited by John Coulson and published in 1964. Next I would mention the seventh and last chapter of *Body as Spirit*, entitled "Toward a Critique of Religious Experience." The chapter anticipates many of the points made more elaborately in *Theology and Political Society*, though the earlier text is more programmatic in character. Then should come the "Introduction" and "Conclusion: What is Left of Christianity?" in *What Is Living, What Is Dead in Christianity Today?* Reference should also be made here to the series of articles, some expository others polemical, on the relation between theology and religious studies (see the bibliography at the end of this volume).

The reason for my constant return to questions concerning the nature and function of theology is that, since my student days, I have regarded theology as my vocation. I use the word "vocation" in the full religious sense. God has called me to be a theologian. When my superiors told me, already in the seminary, that they intended to send me to Rome to do a degree in theology, my vocation to the priesthood took the specific form of a vocation to be a theologian. Now of course I hold that to be a theologian it is not necessary to be a priest. But at that time, even open-minded thinkers like Yves Congar held that theology was a peculiarly priestly learning, preeminently a matter for priests. In my case, the two vocations merged into one, the priestly, let me confess, becoming less and less meaningful as bound up with the obsolete structure of the Church, the theological vocation becoming more and more meaningful as giving voice to the word of God in the language and context of modernity. In writing about theology, its methods and criteria, its various specialties and forms of argumentations, the different publics to which it is addressed and its relation to *praxis*, I have been engaged in a self-critical examination of my own thinking as a Christian, its assumptions and its principles.

If one looks over the programmatic essays I have listed, it will easily become clear that I have never regarded theology as autonomous or self-sufficient. By this I mean that if theology is to realize its nature and fulfill its task it must enter into a reciprocal relation to the culture in which it finds itself. The first of my essays, "Theology and Its Present Task," called for theology to be at the creative centre of contemporary culture. If it were not there entering into relationship with the other cultural elements it would be stagnant. In *Body as Spirit* and *Theology and Political Society*, I endeavoured to relate theology to the modern tradition of criticism stemming from the Enlightenment, passing through the German Idealist to the Marxist critique of ideology and represented today by the critical theory of the Frankfurt School and most notably by the thought of Jürgen Habermas. It is in that sense that I spoke of a critical theology—a theology that was itself engaged in the process of emancipatory reflection, sharing in that way in the project of Enlightenment.

Now I regard the development of a critical theology as a Catholic enterprise in so far as it is a rejection of Protestant fideism. The Protestant way, as exemplified most consistently in our day by Karl Barth, claims a special status for the discourse arising from faith and rejects any dependence of that discourse upon universal conditions of rationality. Contrast that with Lonergan's reply to a remark of Rahner's. Rahner said that Lonergan's method in theology "could be applied to any human science that was fully conscious of itself as depending on the past and looking toward the future." Lonergan replied that he thought that was true, though he himself was working out its application to theology.[1] The structure of knowing was universal for Lonergan. Whatever functions as a cognitive element implies a universalist claim and that universalist claim is implicit in all our claims to reason and truth. I myself do not regard knowledge as foundational, nor would I reduce our spiritual life to a struggle for knowledge, especially self-knowledge, but insofar as we are engaged in knowing, our knowing must satisfy the general conditions of knowing and the requirements of the various forms of knowledge and the method each form demands.

The Catholic tradition has extended the universalist claim implicit in the analysis of the formal conditions of knowledge and modes of rationality to the substantive content of the Catholic belief-system. This gives rise to major questions, circling around exclusivism versus pluralism, universalism versus particularism, certitude versus fallibilism. I have tackled these questions in *Theology and Political Society*, in *What Is Living, What Is Dead in Christianity Today?* and earlier in *Temptations of Religion*. Briefly, I consider the system of Catholic orthodoxy as embodying an indefensible exclusivism, a substitutionalist instead of an interactive universalism, and a claim to certitude incompatible with the fallible character of all human knowledge, including religious knowledge. I have taken the distinction between substitutionalist and interactive universalism from Seyla Benhabib.[2] Substitutionalist universalism identifies the experience of a specific group of subjects as the paradigmatic case of the human as such: interactive universalism acknowledges the plurality of modes of being human and regards difference as a starting point for reflection and action.

The relations between the particular and the universal is the dominant theme in the debates about modernity and postmodernity. Modernity stands for Enlightenment universalism with its trust in reason and truth as capable of making universal validity claims. Postmodernity returns to the particularity of tradition and of the stories constituting the heart of those traditions and insists on the incommensurability of different traditions and cultures. Classicial German philosophy, coming from the Enlightenment, proceeded under the sign of identity: post-Nietzschean philosophy under the sign of difference.

II

I want to look more closely at the relationship between reason and faith in this present epoch, which is commonly referred to as a postmetaphysical, postmodern age.

The Enlightenment was the triumph of a certain kind of rationality. It was the victory of *logos* over *mythos*. The Enlightenment *logos* was an attempt to satisfy a lust for certitude. From Descartes onwards nothing less than demonstrated truth deserved the epithet "rational." Paradoxically enough, this desire for absolute certitude was a confusion of reason with myth.

Human reason is limited and subject to error. The desire for absolute certitude wants to make the transition from *mythos* to *logos* without surrendering the warm certitude of myth.

To put it another way, Enlightenment rationality defended a strong concept of reason. Habermas elaborates this point. The classical metaphysical tradition from Parmenides to Hegel maintains a claim to necessity and totality, which contrasts with the more modest claims made for modern science which has learned to be content for a long time now with a pluralist fallibilism. He sees the reaction of Heidegger, Adorno, and Derrida against the universalism of philosophy as determined by a strong concept of truth, theory and system. These three thinkers are, as it were, still living in the shadow of Hegel. They have not yet come to terms with the fallibilist consciousness of the sciences.[3]

It was in 1973 that I myself made an appeal for fallibilism in the first chapter, "The Lust for Certitude," in *Temptations of Religion*. Richard Bernstein ends his most recent book, *The New Constellation: The Ethical-Political Horizons of Modernity/Postmodernity*, with a quotation from John Courtney Murray, which he sees as expressing an engaged fallibilistic pluralism.[4]

I am arguing, as I have argued for years, for a limited, embodied, fallible human reason. Such a stance may not have the excitement of the rhetoric of postmodernity but the end of a representational epistemology is not the death of truth itself. What is happening is the turning of the critical thrust of Enlightenment reason upon itself. If one goes all the way with Nietzsche then truth loses its meaning and the critical impulse consumes itself. However, it is difficult to see how those who go to that extreme avoid a performative contradiction. If we engage in critique, how can we avoid making some affirmation, if only concerning the norms implied in critique itself?[5]

One way of covering over the absence of a truth-affirmation, together with the performative contradiction this carries with it, is by merging philosophy and literature. This moves the critique of reason into the domain of rhetoric. Philosophical thinking is no longer concerned with solving problems or answering questions with the production of affirmations.[6]

It is not difficult to harmonize religious faith and fallibilism. What is needed in order to do so is a distinction between faith and beliefs. Faith is the fundamental religious response. It is an orientation towards unlimited reality as accepted in a transcendent response or movement of unrestricted love. This faith-love is divine revelation in the primary sense of the presence of divine reality in our minds and hearts. As a fundamental response or originating idea, faith-love gives rise to a body of religious beliefs, constituting a tradition. The absoluteness associated with our religious response belongs to faith-love, not to doctrines. That absoluteness of faith should not be confused with a certitude of belief. Doctrines are marked by a relativity, mutability and cultural limitation of all products of human finite intelligence, however illumined. A recognition that all human knowledge is fallible, subject to error, does not destroy religion either in its theoretical or in its practical functioning.

Quite otherwise is the effect of seeing religious discourse as belonging to the domain of rhetoric and therefore making no truth claim. This identification of religion and literature would seem to be incompatible with the meaning and function of both religious faith and religious beliefs.

Nevertheless, a recent attempt has been made to combine a rejection of universalist reason with its truth claims with Christian faith and belief. This is being presented as a movement of theology into postmodernity. I am referring to John Milbank's *Theology and Social Theory: Beyond Secular Reason*.[7] Milbank speaks of "secular reason," and when he plays out its meaning he identifies it with "liberal politics, political economy, sociology and Hegelianism-Marxism."[8] For him secular reason embodies an ontology of power and conflict. That ontology cannot be refuted, because it is only a *mythos*, but Christianity itself is only a *mythos*. Hence the issue between them cannot be settled by argument or dialectics but only by persuasion or rhetoric. Each must try to out-narrate the other. The one who tells the better story gains the laurel.[9] In this postmodern, post-Nietzschean era all suppositions about transcendence, Milbank declares, are ungrounded and mutually incommensurable. Paradoxically this exercise in skeptical relativism combines with a strong affirmation of the Christian meta-narrative as an ontology of peace and with an exclusivist understanding of the Christian Church as indispensable.[10] Secular theory is regarded as modern nihilism, and "between nihilistic univocity and Catholic analogy (which includes the convertibility of truth, beauty and goodness) there is no longer any third liberal path."[11]

I remain unpersuaded by Milbank's presentation of his own thought. At the beginning of his book he sees himself as engaged in a twofold task. First, the demolition of modern secular social theory from a Christian perspective. The assumptions governing that theory correspond to the rejection or modification of orthodox Christian positions. Neither the Christian positions nor their rejections are rationally justifiable. The persuading of Christian theologians to appropriate the Christian positions for reasons intrinsic to the Christian *logos*, not by the mediation of a universal human reason. Now I find it highly implausible and unpersuasive to suppose that the complex set of considerations put forward by Milbank is in the last analysis a matter of rhetoric or indeed of "literary taste."[12] Theology as public discourse must appeal to methods and modes of rational argumentation and rules of evidence. A small point: in the Introduction Milbank says he will argue against the secular theorists but later on he dismisses MacIntyre's wanting to argue against secular reason. It would be difficult for Milbank to make his performance correspond to his theoretical statements. Reason is not so easily banished.

What is unexpected is that Milbank turns to the French Catholic philosopher Maurice Blondel, the philosopher of the supernatural, in support of his postmodern perspectivism, pragmatism and historicism, and for a postmodern regaining of the supernatural.[13] Contrary to Bondel's explicit understanding of his own work, Milbank maintains that Blondel's philosophy must be reunderstood as theology.[14] So rethought, it is perhaps "the boldest exercise in Christian thought of modern times."[15]

It would be out of place here to enter into a detailed interpretation of Blondel's thought. There are, however, two points where Blondel's work may suggest a relationship between religious thought and postmodernity. First, the primacy of action; second, the impossibility of separating the contribution of the natural and the supernatural in the concrete life and thought of human beings. I should like to develop these two points, though without claiming that they represent the thought of Blondel himself.

In matters of action, faith may precede reason. It can do so because knowledge is not foundational. What is foundational is love. Faith as distinct from beliefs is love. Hence the absoluteness of faith. Faith is the drive towards transcendence, the thrust of human beings out of and beyond themselves, out of and beyond all the limited orders and human certainties under which they live. The absoluteness of faith is the absoluteness of total demand and total response in an experience of unrestricted love. So on the level of action, faith-love comes first and precedes the critique of reason. Iris Marion Young makes a similar point. She writes:

As I understand the implications of Kristeva's approach to language, it entails that communication is not only motivated by the aim to reach consensus, a shared understanding of the world, but also and even more basically by a desire to love and be loved. Modulations of eros operate in the semiotic elements of communication that put the subject's identity in question in relation to itself, its own past and imagination, and to others, in the heterogeneity of their identity. People do not merely hear, take in and argue about the validity of utterances. Rather they are affected, in an immediate and felt fashion, by the other's expression and its manner of being addressed to us.[16]

The function of reason as critique applies to faith and beliefs. There is no "no-go" area from which we exclude matters of religion. At the same time, reason does not give rise to faith. Faith and beliefs do not come from argument or the exercise of abstract reasoning. A thesis of Blondel is that the product and consequences of action always exceed the input of the human agent because God is present in the action so that its product and consequences must be measured not only in relation to human agency but also to divine agency.

The second line of reflection concerns the inexplicable intertwining of natural and supernatural in the concrete life and history of human beings. In concrete, historical humanity, there is no possibility of separating the natural from the supernatural. Thus, in social and political life one cannot establish a purely natural or secular order. Political and social achievements will reflect the empowerment given by God's grace; the failure to overcome destructive forces ravaging society will reflect human sin. The modern state is a transformed church that could not have emerged historically without the contribution of Christianity. So F.D. Maurice, quoted by Nicholls, can say: "The State is as much God's creation as the Church."

The word "supernatural" is off putting because it has the wrong association. One could speak instead of a transgressive or transforming experience. The point is that human life and history do not proceed tranquilly on a single level. It embraces subversive or diremptive experiences. From Hegel onwards modern thought has assumed we live in a state of division, disruption and alienation. Hegel claimed that the task and achievement of philosophy is to bring about reconciliation. The fact, however, is that Enlightenment reason has proved itself incapable of fulfilling its promise to usher in both personal and social integration. Hegel's assumption that integrative reconciliation could be achieved in thought has proved illusory.

In his contribution to the collection, *Habermas, Modernity and Public Theology*, Habermas asks "What separates the internal perspective of theology from the external perspective of those who enter into a dialogue with theology?"[17] The theological answer would be the active presence of God, which is carried forward on the vehicle of human action.

To ignore the supernatural is in effect to ignore much of the data needed to elaborate a sound social theory. Milbank is right thus far in seeing the Enlightenment social theory as a covert, distorted theology; in other words, an heretical formation.

III

I have unsystematically been musing upon the present state of theology, with a view to anticipating its future. I have done so as an expression of gratitude to those who have honoured me with the volume. I find myself in substantial agreement with their comments upon my work. What is perhaps more important is that they all share an orientation towards the concrete and historical which makes them proponents of a theology for tomorrow.

Notes

1   Philip McShane, "An Interview with Fr. Bernard Lonergan, S.J.," *The Clergy Review* 56 (1971): 413.

2   Seyla Benhabib, "The Generalized and the Concrete Other: The Kohlberg-Gilligan Controversy and Feminist Theory," in Seyla Benhabib and Drucilla Cornell, eds., *Feminism as Critique* (Cambridge: Polity Press, 1987), 81.

3   Jürgen Habermas, *The Philosophical Discourse of Modernity* (Cambridge, MA: MIT Press, 1987), 408-409.

4   Richard J. Bernstein, *The New Constellation: The Ethical-Political Horizons of Modernity/Postmodernity* (Cambridge, MA: MIT Press, 1992), 339.

5   Ibid., 326.

6   Habermas, *The Philosophical Discourse of Modernity*, 210.

7   Oxford: Basil Blackwell, 1990.

8   Ibid., 326.

9   Ibid., 279-80; 330-31.

10   Ibid., 387-88.

11   Ibid., 318.

12   Ibid., 330.

13   Ibid., 218-19.

14   Ibid., 217.

15   Ibid.

16   Iris Marion Young, "Impartiality and the Civic Republic: Some Implications of Feminist Critique of Moral and Political Theory," in Benhabib and Cornell, eds., *Feminism as Critique*, 72.

17   Jürgen Habermas, "Transcendence from Within, Transcendence in This World," in Don S. Browning and Francis Shüssler Fiorenza, eds., *Habermas, Modernity, and Public Theology* (New York: Crossroad, 1992), 231.

Two

For Whom Do We Write?
The Responsibility of the Theologian

PAUL LAKELAND

I

In recent years in the Catholic Church the role and ecclesial identity of the theologian has become a thorny issue.[1] I would like to address this question by examining the various audiences that the theologian's work might be thought to address. For whom, in fact, does the theologian write? Is our audience something so nebulous as "the Church," or the "Catholic community?" Is it the "academy?" Is it perhaps, as the institution would certainly have us believe, the magisterium, which at least argues that it needs the help of professional theologians to accomplish the task of teaching with authority? Is the audience for which the theologian writes an ecclesial subgroup of theologically literate folk? And don't some theologians write for one group, some for another, and some for a mixture of two or more?

An important early voice in this discussion was that of Charles Davis. In *A Question of Conscience*,[2] Davis stressed his independence of ecclesial institutions in such a way that one can only describe him as a freelance theologian. Most others who share many of his views have not taken that path, but have asserted their independence from within.[3] As a matter of fact, most theologians will probably continue to do their work in one or another recognizable ecclesial community. But independence of any authoritarian watchdog is highly useful and necessary to the theologian, even if it is an independence of spirit rather than of formal affiliation. Consequently, Davis may be viewed as a model for the practice and self-understanding for what has increasingly been called "the age of the lay theologian."

In the years since *A Question of Conscience*, a number of issues have become clearer. Four factors in particular in the current situation of theologians in the Church set the stage for a consideration of the theologian's self-understanding. After briefly examining these, I shall turn for help to insights of Walter Benjamin, Antonio Gramsci, and Edward Said, while remaining in dialogue with the work of Davis. I shall try to defend three theses about the theologian's place in the ecclesial community. First, I shall argue that the theologian must, in order to do authentic theology, be concretely independent of those who control the means of production. Secondly, I shall defend the claim that the theologian is best conceived of on the model of Gramsci's "organic intellectual," conscious of the need for universal hermeneutical suspicion and committed to shaking the people free of the current hegemony. Finally, I shall argue that a theologian must avoid the monocentric tendencies of most theology, and seek to do a kind of "secular" theology.

II

Four related factors seem to make the ecclesial significance of theologians in today's Church so intensely problematic. In the first place, the Catholic tradition has come to recognize that not all theologians are ordained ministers, and that the roles of teacher, preacher, and theologian are shared out among different but overlapping groups. It is, however, bound to the clumsy belief that there is no necessary connection between theological learning and teaching authority. In the strictest sense, only bishops teach, while on even the most generous of assessments, many bishops could not be accounted theologians. Preaching is reserved to ordained ministers—bishops, priests, and deacons—all of whom proclaim the gospel under the watchful eye of the magisterium. Theologians, of course, may be and often are ordained ministers, but many are not, and ordination is thus not proper to the role of theologian—unless, that is, nonordained theologians be understood not to be theologians in the fullest sense of the word.[4] How a theologian's work relates to and interrelates with that of the bishop or the preacher, in consequence, is not self-evident. In terms of the question of audience, is the theologian *primarily and properly* addressing the bishops, as the official teachers, or the whole believing community, or the academy of other theologians and interested scholars, or the world at large?

A second and more trivial matter, though one which often clouds the issue and which follows directly from the first, is that theologians now don't look like theologians then. They may be laypeople, they may be women, they may even be Chinese. They may have PhDs, God help us, from the University of Chicago. They very likely work in contexts where the possession of the "canonical mission" is not an issue. None of these things in themselves make them better or worse scholars or more or less faithful members of the believing community than Father X with an STD from the Gregorian University. But truth to tell, the institutional Church in at least the last few centuries never seems to have envisaged the possibility that its male clerical theologians might come to be outnumbered by such as these. This unpreparedness for the kinds of theologians who have crept upon us is reflected in the few recent documents of the Church which touch on theology and theologians. Variations on the old clerical theme are either ignored or overlooked.[5]

In the third place, many theologians today work with a whole variety of disciplines and in an intellectual milieu that those who possess more traditional understandings of their roles find it difficult to recognize. All would more or less agree that deeper reflection on the tradition and a more sensitive reading of it in the light of the times are among theologians' principal tasks. But it is not always evident to representatives of the institutional Church how extensive use of the writings of Marx, Weber, Freud, Nietzsche, Derrida, Foucault, Wittgenstein, Kristeva, or even Mary Daly contribute to the fulfillment of these responsibilities.

Fourthly and finally, the work of theologians today is not always conducted with primary reference to recent doctrinal formulations or clarifications. The theologian, in other words, is not always in direct dialogue with what the magisterium tends to see as the tradition. Theologians range more widely these days than perhaps they once did, while the magisterium continues, as perhaps it must, to be concerned solely with the particular tradition. While a tradition and a community remain important and even perhaps normative for the identity of the particular theologian, the tradition itself can no longer be considered by many theologians to be normative in any more absolute sense of the term. Not only ecumenism, but also and lately far more importantly, the dialogue of world religions that goes by the name of the "theology of religions" represents the abandonment, on the part of theologians, of the traditional kinds of claims to ultimacy.[6]

III

In his essay "The Author as Producer,"[7] Walter Benjamin was taken up with two issues which shed light on our particular concern. First, he addressed the role of the revolutionary writer, and the tension between a concern for the political correctness of the opinions expressed, and the artist's need, as a matter of integrity, to seek literary quality. Against the standard dogmatic assertion that "a work that shows the correct political tendency need show no other quality," Benjamin countered: "a work that exhibits the correct tendency must of necessity have every other quality."[8] Second, he looked at what structural situation a writer needed in order to guard the authenticity of her or his words. In striving to adjudicate this in the context of a materialist analysis, he suggested that the important consideration is not the attitudes a work expresses towards the relations of production of its time, but the position it occupies vis-à-vis these relations. So, generalizing somewhat, "the place of the intellectual in the class struggle can be identified, or better, chosen, only on the basis of his position in the process of production."[9]

It is not necessary to adopt Benjamin's theoretical framework, or to subject the institutional Church to the kind of class analysis that it would roundly condemn, for it to be possible to point to similarities between the place of the politically progressive writer in society and the place of the theologian in a pre-modern Church. The former is struggling for the honest expression of a commitment to political transformation in a world in which so many of the means of disseminating those ideas are under the control of those who do not share the commitment. Many Catholic theologians are in an analogous situation, profoundly unhappy with numerous elements of institutional ecclesial practice at the present time, for sound theological reasons, but conscious that power remains in the hands of the official representatives of the institution. Those who work within Church-controlled institutions may, if they speak their minds, lose their party cards: those who work more independently are not taken particularly seriously.

If we take Benjamin's two points consecutively, then the first involves us in looking for the ecclesial analogies to a tension between ideological purity and intellectual integrity. These analogies are not long in the discovering. The Congregation for the Doctrine of the Faith (CDF) is the institution's watchdog of correct ideological tendency, and it is clear to that body how such a tension must be resolved.[10] The individual may not

,indulge in any show of public disagreement or dissent, but must rather seek to cultivate a "religious submission of will and intellect."[11] Final inability to accept the teaching of the magisterium must be met with a willingness "to suffer for the truth, in silence and prayer."[12] And what else could be the outcome, when any disagreement "could not be justified if it were based solely upon the fact that the validity of the given teaching is not evident or upon the opinion that the opposite position would be the more probable"?[13] If this is not convincing, then to clinch the matter, the theologian's hermeneutical rules must include "the principle which affirms that magisterial teaching, by virtue of divine assistance, has a validity beyond its argumentation."[14] One is tempted to ask why the divine assistance wasn't extended to the argumentation.

In the face of such a magisterial self-interpretation, the theologian of integrity is forced to choose between the silence that inevitably betokens consent and the public act of writing that might bring rejection (or a semisecret trial and a call for self-criticism). There is nothing fanciful here about the parallel to the methods of totalitarian societies, and Benjamin's axiom also retains its validity: "a work that exhibits the correct tendency must of necessity have every other quality." Seek ye first the truth, we might paraphrase this, and correctness shall be added unto ye. In other words, no consideration of any kind whatsoever absolves the theologian from the duty to follow the search for truth wherever it shall lead. Every intellectual worker, of course, needs to preserve humility about the conclusions to which he or she seems to have arrived and to remain flexible and open to change. But this does not and cannot mean that conclusions that seem to differ from the positions of official teaching must *ipso facto* be abandoned.

If the theologian's search for truth must be uncompromising yet humble, and if the magisterium must walk a fine line between its responsibility to protect the tradition and its inclination in the defense of the tradition to adopt a kind of "national security" ideology, then how can the two sides come together? As I have suggested elsewhere, the paradigm must be that of a conversation to which all have equal access, and which is open-ended and directed towards a consensus about norms for action.[15] Moreover, the role of the bishops *qua bishops* ought to be perceived more as arbiters of fair play in the dialogue. Tradition as discourse must have rules of fair play, and these rules must be enforced by someone.[16]

The Christian tradition in general, and the Catholic community since the Second Vatican Council, has begun to converge on the idea that the Church

is a community whose historical reality is a pilgrim-like search for the
fullness of truth, not a confident celebration of its possession. So the
theologian's search for truth, if conducted sincerely and without arrogance,
is entirely consonant with ecclesial reality. The fidelity of the theologian, like
everyone else in the ecclesial community, must be interpreted as commitment
to a process, not to a series of formulations. Primary among the forms of
unfaithfulness, clearly, would be any attempts to deny the dynamic character
of the community by insisting upon the subordination of this historical
process—within which must be counted the intellectual endeavours of
theologians—to a static, unhistorical vision of Church doctrine.

Much the same point was made extremely well in Davis's *A Question of
Conscience*, when he wrote that the Church as a social structure fails to be
a "zone of truth,"[17] and that this failure is a "corrupting influence upon the
whole social structure of the Church."[18] The impact upon theologians is
that some "become adept at knowing how much they can get away with,"
while others "become victims of the system," using "earnest but biassed
arguments . . . to defend the system."[19] Davis sums up his attitude in words
that, while strong, would be echoed by many theologians today:

> The question is what attitude to truth is manifested as prevalent in the
> Church. It seems to me that truth is used, not respected or sought,
> doctrine is held in the manner of a prejudice not as truth, words and
> arguments are not handled to discover and communicate truth but
> manipulated as a means of power to support an authoritative system: in
> brief, that truth is subordinated to authority, not authority put at the
> service of truth.[20]

Turning to Benjamin's second concern, it seems clear then that the
appropriate situation of the theologian who values the freedom to serve the
Church with integrity is one of independence of the means of production.
Here Benjamin's materialist analysis is particularly illuminating. What counts
for Benjamin are not the opinions the writer expresses but the actual concrete
relations of the writer to the means of production, that is, to those who hold
power. Translating this into ecclesial terms leads to a rather startling
conclusion. Contrary to the normal institutional understanding, the possession
of a canonical mission, or at least work done under the aegis of such a
mission, which the CDF itself recognizes as "a participation in the work of
the magisterium,"[21] would be less likely to lead to authentic theologizing

than that conducted more independently. Catholic theology in North America would certainly seem to bear this out. It is to the liberal arts colleges and the major Catholic universities, whose theologians for the most part do not possess the canonical mission, that one needs to look to find most of the more creative theological work. While a number of possible explanations of this state of affairs might suggest themselves, it seems undeniable that independence and creativity go together.

While independence of the means of production may mean greater freedom for theological creativity, it is not without its problems. Indeed, it raises in particularly acute form the question of a criteriology for the Catholicity of any theologian. If the theologian is not an "official" theologian, and yet intends her or his work as a contribution to the enrichment of the Catholic tradition, how is this individual's claim to be a Catholic theologian to be tested? On the one hand, it does not seem to me that I am a Catholic theologian because an authoritarian watchdog says that I am orthodox, or that I am orthodox because I am in the possession of a canonical mission. On the other hand, I am not enriching the tradition merely because I say I am. But then who decides what constitutes faithful theologizing? If the magisterial approach is far too narrow, is the only alternative to have no criteria at all? Or do we perhaps need to look to some non-judgmental form of recognition by the community as a dialogue-partner, even a dialogue-leader, in the search for truth that should distinguish the Church? And if this is so, is it possible to find a role again for a magisterium that recognizes its peculiar authority in the teaching process while rejecting its severely authoritarian self-understanding? We already touched on this above, in envisaging bishops as arbiters of the process of discourse that ought to constitute the living tradition of the community. The question will reemerge towards the end of our discussion of Antonio Gramsci.

IV

Antonio Gramsci's work on the role of the intellectuals in society[22] begins by attempting to destroy one of their major illusions. Traditional intellectuals assume, says Gramsci, that they are independent of the dominant social group, whereas in fact they are an essential part of the dominant group. They perform an indispensable function on behalf of whichever class happens currently to be dominant. They assist, however unthinkingly, in the maintenance of "hegemony." Gramsci's notion of hegemony, a sophisticated add-on to Marx's concept of ideology, stresses the need for the free consent of the masses to the form of life and ideology espoused by the dominant group, if its ideology is to be successfully imposed. "Hegemony" is thus the system of domination as and when it is embraced as liberative by those who are actually oppressed by it. Needless to say, such a notion has wide significance even in states that espouse a rhetoric of democracy and freedom, since such language may itself be a prime example of hegemony.

Traditional intellectuals are those who reject the idea that they represent a class or class interests; indeed, who argue for the nonideological character of the intellectual life, and who claim that the search for truth is untouched by political considerations. In our own times a prime example of such people would be those who maintain the nonideological, noncoercive character of the "canon" of the Western tradition. Gramsci makes the somewhat obvious point that because such people claim to be ideology-free, and perhaps even try to be, therefore they are inevitably if unconsciously representatives of the ideology of the status quo, that is, of the dominant social group.

What Gramsci wants to see is the transformation of the traditional intellectual into the "organic intellectual," that is, into one who is aware of the ideological underpinnings of the particular opinions he or she expresses. This advance to a critical self-understanding is to be achieved through a "dialectic between intellectuals and the masses" which culminates in the identity of theory and praxis. So the organic intellectual will resist hegemony and identify with those who are its victims, both learning from them and leading them to a form of conscientization in which they will no longer embrace their own oppression as if it were their emancipation, but will seek their own real interests.

Gramsci's idea of the organic intellectual transfers smoothly to an institution like the Catholic Church,[23] which proclaims a message of freedom and emancipation while employing an extremely authoritarian self-understanding. The Catholic Church in particular operates as a hegemony, not, of course, in its annunciation of the liberative force of the gospel, but by proclaiming the normative character of its own role in the proclamation of that gospel. This claim to ultimacy, a misplaced ultimacy, is still taken for granted by the vast majority of Catholics. But are they not thereby shoring up the system that precludes their own full exposure to the liberating power of the gospel?

What happens if we replace Gramsci's investigation of the intellectual's role in society with our own consideration of the theologian's place in the community of faith? Gramsci's traditional and organic intellectuals are paralleled in the Church by two kinds of theologians. One group is the "Church-theologians," those who embrace and give intellectual respectability to the institutional hegemony. Exactly as the CDF would recommend, they subject their own work to the institutional tests of orthodoxy. They imagine they are avoiding factionalism and partiality, ascribing that vice to those who dissent here or there. But like Gramsci's traditional intellectuals they are (perhaps unwitting) tools of the ecclesial hegemony. The second group, of "organic theologians," recognizes that all positions, including their own *and* the official position of the institution, must be subject to the exercise of hermeneutical suspicion. In particular, they would consider their primary allegiance to be to the community of faith rather than to the institution. In dialogue with that community, they would seek to develop a critical consciousness among the believers that would lead them in an ever more nuanced manner towards their own emancipation. A "fidelity of obedience" to an institution could not be recognized as an appropriate posture of anyone living in the freedom of the children of God.

A related division of the theological task is suggested by Davis in *Theology and Political Society*,[24] where he derives from Habermas a classification of theology into historical, hermeneutical and critical varieties. The third, critical form must be added on to the other two, he believes, if critical self-reflection can be accounted a moment within faith itself. This critical theology would have two tasks: "the formation and development of a critical theory of society and history," and the initiation of "the process of self-reflection with the Christian community."[25] Critical theology would then be the work of those within the community who acknowledge the applicability of ideology critique to the Church, by the Church. For myself, I would have to express the hope that even historical and hermeneutical theologies would have within them a moment of critique, that is, that they would be politically self-conscious. One irrefutable contribution of feminist theology, for example, has been to show how intensely critical can be the retrieval of Christian origins conducted through historical and hermeneutical means. In other words, in a blend of Davis and Gramsci, even the historical and hermeneutical varieties of theology would have to be conducted by organic, not traditional, theologians.

Gramsci's idea of the organic intellectual is clearly helpful in handling the question with which the previous section of this paper concluded. If the theologian's value is not to be self-assigned nor to consist in an official seal of approval, then perhaps it is to be found in the dialectical discourse between the theologian and the believing community. The relationship of the theologian to the base Christian community as functioning in the Latin American theology of liberation presents just such a picture. The theologian has a certain professional training that the non-theologian simply does not possess. But the theology of liberation done by the community is articulated through the work of the professional, not created by the professional and imposed on the community. Together, they reinforce one another's faithful service of the gospel. Moreover, the example of liberation theology, with its insistence on the "preferential option for the poor," on living in solidarity with and learning from the poor as a precondition for sharing in their work of theological reflection, helps overcome one of the imponderables of Gramsci's idea of the organic intellectual: how can individuals make themselves into representatives of social classes from which they did not emerge in the first place?

The role of bishops in ecclesial discourse can also be illuminated through the example of liberation theology. At its best, and especially in Brazil, bishops, like theologians, have been listeners and learners, participants in the dialogue who have come to understand that their responsibility for overseeing the Church does not mean that they cannot leave a great deal more space for the process of theological reflection to take place in the hands of ordinary members of the believing community. But this idea may be clarified more by the discussion of Edward Said.

V

The role of the best "worldly" criticism, says Said, is to oppose "monocentrism," a concept he understands as "working in conjunction with ethnocentrism, which licenses a culture to cloak itself in the particular authority of certain values over others."[26] Monocentric discourse is "religious" in the worst sense of this word, evidenced in an attachment to "some version of theory liberated from the human and the circumstantial."[27] This doubtless follows Croce's understanding of religion as "a conception of the world which has become a norm of life," and Gramsci's version—"a unity of faith between a conception of the world and a corresponding norm of conduct."[28] Any stress on the private and hermetic as opposed to the public and social "must also be viewed as being part of the same curious veering toward the religious," which Said thinks "expresses an ultimate preference for the secure protection of systems of belief and not for critical activity or consciousness."[29] So criticism is blind to its affiliations with the political world, and the modern critic who was once an intellectual "has become a cleric in the worst sense of the word."[30] "How their discourse can once again collectively become a truly secular enterprise," concludes Said, is "the most serious question critics can be asking one another."[31]

It is not hard for the present-day theologian to find considerable value in Said's assessment of the world of criticism for shedding light on the theological task. In the first place, there are parallels between the monocentric discourse of literary criticism and that of the institutional Church. In both, there is a thirst for narrowness and certainty, which Said dates to the advent of the New Criticism four decades ago, and which the Catholic theologian would have to see as having been more or less prevalent throughout the recent life of the Church, perhaps with the expectation of a relatively heady decade immediately after the end of the Second Vatican Council. In both, there is a new attachment to political neoconservatism. Both reject the attempt to view their positions politically. Both prefer "impenetrable, deliberately obscure, wilfully illogical" languages. Neither can tolerate the open-ended, civil and humane yet committed discourse of the radicalized Enlightenment.

The greater value of Said lies in elucidating the theologian's self-understanding. The critical theologian, then, to return to the terminology of Davis discussed earlier, needs to insist—like her literary critical counterpart—on the fact that she is engaged in "a truly secular enterprise," that is, that there is no pre-set monocentric cultural interpretation tying her hands in the search for truth. Rather, theology is "contentious knowledge,"[32] concerned not only with the careful reading of texts (the hermeneutic and historical) but above all with "the force of statements in texts."[33] Said, in insisting on this being true of criticism, has at heart a concern to overcome the isolation of criticism, its tendency in its "religious" form to view itself as "an isolated paddock" and to indulge in "the harmless rhetoric of self-delighting humanism."[34] In transposing the insight into theology and religion proper, however, the tendency is not so much for religion to consider itself an isolated field, as to consider itself on a level, serene and unassailable, above every field and paddock whatsoever.

The self-isolation of religion on its own plane, its "religiousness" in Said's language, can be pinned to the traditional claims of a religion of revelation. The revealed truth that the community possesses sets its claims and its certainties apart from all other fields of endeavour, and from all other religious claims. Davis tackles this issue head-on in his book, *What Is Living, What Is Dead in Christianity Today?* arguing that the continuing value of Christianity is in direct proportion to the degree to which it is ready to abandon its claims to "the definitive, literal, and exclusive truth about God, humankind, and the universe."[35] In other words, Davis as a critical theologian is practising and advocating *secular* rather than *religious* criticism, in the sense that he avoids the evil of monocentrism. However, if the critical theologian is to be distinguishable from the social critic, the object of his or her "secular" criticism remains the community of faith, its unfolding tradition, and the world in which it seeks the truth.

While Davis seems to me to overstate the degree to which Christians in general are able to abandon the uniqueness of the claims of their religious tradition, it is true that very many theologians would be extremely reluctant to continue to claim this kind of normativity or ultimacy. To the extent that this is the case, the theologian's view of her task must become radically different. In particular, it would be difficult to understand how the primary audience of the theologian could be a magisterium which, as Davis points out, clings to the myth even after the breaking of the myth, unless a particularly self-sacrificial theologian conceived of it as her or his vocation to alert the bishops to the profound error of their ways. Much more likely, the theologian will choose to address directly those whom the magisterium seeks to protect by keeping them in ignorance. The ideology of exclusive, revealed truth is a particularly seductive form of monocentrism, and the critical theologian's task in today's world may very well be to break it. That way may lie the freedom of the gospel. This does *not* mean that every word of the theologian is addressed directly as a challenge to the ideology, but that all the work of the theologian starts from the kind of modified ultimacy that can make room for the complementary wisdom of other religious traditions.

VI

Towards the end of *What Is Living, What Is Dead in Christianity Today?*, Davis takes David Tracy to task for idealizing the notion of a public.[36] For Tracy, thinks Davis, a public is simply "a reference group, an addressee of theology." So for example, Tracy believes that the public to which systematic theology is addressed is the Church. But as Davis points out, the Catholic Church possesses no public, in the sense of "a community of discourse, exercising a surveillance and critique over the teaching and action of those holding authority within it."[37] This point has been made repeatedly in the present paper: the appropriate question is not that of the *addressee* of theology, but of the *audience* of theology, that is, the one who will listen, who can receive the work of the theologian. The censorious listening of the magisterium does not count, but can we in fact be any more confident that the community as a whole constitutes an audience? Can a community kept in the dark so long be relied upon to possess enough knowledge or theological sense to constitute an actual, concrete and historical "public"?

It may in the end be that the critical theologians, or the historical/hermeneutical theologians in the critical movement, must learn to think of themselves on the model of the social critic as outlined in Michael Walzer's recent book, *The Company of Critics*.[38] The critical theologian, like Walzer's social critic, must hold a mirror up to society and force it to look, must "question relentlessly the platitudes and myths" of the community, and express the aspiration of the people.[39] Like the social critic, he or she must embrace two limitations to the exercise of such a vocation: the inevitable partiality and subjectivity of viewpoint, and the chance that those before whom the mirror is held do not share the theologian's moral references. While we can criticize everything, we can do it only from our own particular standpoint, and there are as many mirrors as there are social critics or critical theologians. Such a pluralism is healthy, but the second limitation is less so. A moral sensitivity cannot coerce others; that is why it is more likely to be the possession of victim than oppressor. So the critical theologian—in a parallelism to the life of Jesus that some may find heartening—may be destined to fail in the attempt to provide a recipe for emancipation. But then, in Walzer's words, "hope" is "the one common mark of the critical enterprise."

The theologian, in conclusion, writes for the whole Church as community, out of what Walzer calls a "benevolence," a concern for and commitment to the good of the community, recognizing that its continuing significance must lie in passing beyond those limitations which it has understandably inherited from the past, but seems to want to cling to in the present. The audience of the theologian, in the sense discussed above, is for the time being relatively small. Aside from other theologians, it can only be those people, members of the community or not, with the confidence and openness to face a future that will be radically different from the past, if it is to exist at all. The theologian's task is to criticize and cajole, to be committed but not dogmatic, and to face the likelihood of failure. In the recent history of English-speaking theology, it seems clear there is no better example of such a critical theologian, or theologian as ecclesial critic, than Charles Davis.

Notes

1   Three valuable studies of the ecclesial role of the theologian, each quite different in approach from the others, are: Nicholas Lash, "Criticism or Construction? The Task of the Theologian," in *Theology on the Way to Emmaus* (London: SCM Press, 1986), 3-17; William May, ed., *Vatican Authority and American Catholic Dissent* (New York: Crossroad, 1989); and John E. Thiel, *Imagination and Authority: Theological Authorship in the Modern Tradition* (Minneapolis: Fortress Press, 1991).

2   New York: Harper & Row, 1967.

3   There may be a theologians' parallel here to the examination of young Catholics' relations to the Church in Eugene Kennedy's recent book, *Tomorrow's Catholics, Yesterday's Church: The Two Cultures of American Catholicism* (New York: Harper & Row, 1988). Of course, it remains an open question whether such a position, adopted either by theologians or by young Catholics, is intellectually honest, or whether—as Davis would have wanted to maintain in *A Question of Conscience*—ought to lead them out of the Church.

4   Some, for example, distinguish between two kinds of theologians, "official" theologians and those who pursue theology as "personal research," essentially a kind of theological hobbyist. For this strange and to my mind alarming and demeaning distinction, see Otto Semmelroth, S.J., and Karl Lehmann, "The Ecclesial Magisterium and Theology," in Charles E. Curran and Richard A. McCormick, S.J., eds., *Readings in Moral Theology No. 3: The Magisterium and Morality* (Ramsey, NY: Paulist Press, 1982), 151-70. The article consists of theses on the topic prepared for and approved by the International Theological Commission, together with a brief commentary by the authors. The distinction between theology "as an official exercise" and theology as personal research occurs in the commentary to thesis 7, 166.

5   An extremely helpful document in illuminating this issue is the "Report of the Catholic Theological Society of America Committee on the Profession of Faith and the Oath of Fidelity," April 15, 1990. If, as seems reasonable to suppose, those who are

expected to take the oath of fidelity and make the profession of faith are the same people to whom a canonical mission is extended, then the CTSA's discussion makes clear that most American theologians, who as a matter of fact teach outside ecclesiastical institutions in the narrow sense of the word, do not possess a canonical mission, since they cannot be held to the oath and profession of faith. The CTSA concludes that Canon 833's focus upon "teachers in any universities whatsoever who teach disciplines which deal with faith or morals" cannot be construed to affect non-Catholics, Catholics teaching in state universities or secular institutions, or any institution, however professedly Catholic. In each of these cases it cannot be said that "competent ecclesiastical authority has established [it], governs it, and could close it" (62). Thus, most of those who consider themselves Catholic theologians are scarcely envisaged in official considerations of the strictures that bind theologians.

6   Rethinking the role of religion in an age when its claims to be normative for the whole of human history no longer carry conviction is the ultimate purpose of Charles Davis's book, *What Is Living, What Is Dead in Christianity Today?* (San Francisco: Harper & Row, 1986), though this only emerges clearly in the final chapter. More will be said later in the paper about this important issue.

7   Walter Benjamin, *Reflections: Essays, Aphorisms, Autobiographical Writings*, ed. Peter Demetz (New York: Harcourt, Brace, Jovanovich, 1978), 220-38.

8   Ibid., 221.

9   Ibid., 228.

10   See "Instruction on the Ecclesial Vocation of the Theologian," *Origins* 20, no.8 (July 5 1990): 117, 119-27. (Hereafter cited as *EVT.*)

11   Ibid., 23.

12   Ibid., 31.

13   Ibid., 28.

14   Ibid., 34.

15   See my *Theology and Critical Theory: The Discourse of the Church* (Nashville: Abingdon Press, 1990).

16   Ibid., 159-74.

17   Davis, *Question*, 71.

18   Ibid., 74.

19   Ibid., 75.

20   Ibid., 76.

21   *EVT*, 22.

22   *Selections from the "Prison Notebooks,"* ed. Quintin Hoare and Geoffrey Nowell Smith (New York: International Publishers, 1971), especially 3-23.

23   To my knowledge, two authors have preceded me in the application of Gramsci's idea of the organic intellectual in the field of religion. Neither of them, however, is concerned with the particular use which I wish to make. See Cornel West, *Prophesy Deliverance: An Afro-American Revolutionary Christianity* (Philadelphia: Westminster Press, 1982); and Bradford E. Hinze, *Doctrinal Criticism, Reform and Development*

in the Work of Friedrich Schleiermacher and Johann Sebastian Drey (PhD diss., University of Chicago, 1989), 210-32.

24 Cambridge: Cambridge University Press, 1980, 72-74.

25 Ibid., 73.

26 Edward Said, *The World, the Text and the Critic* (Cambridge, MA: Harvard University Press, 1983), 53.

27 Ibid., 291.

28 See the interesting discussion of this in David McLellan, *Marxism and Religion* (New York: Harper & Row, 1987), 115.

29 Said, *The World and the Text*, 291.

30 Ibid.

31 Ibid., 292.

32 Ibid., 224, utilizing an insight of Foucault, though Said of course is talking about criticism in general.

33 Ibid.

34 Ibid., 225.

35 Davis, *What Is Living*, 122.

36 Tracy's discussion of the three publics of theology is to be found in *The Analogical Imagination: Christian Theology and the Culture of Pluralism* (London: SCM Press, 1981), 6-31.

37 Davis, *What Is Living*, 103.

38 Michael Walzer, *The Company of Critics: Social Criticism and Political Commitment in the Twentieth Century* (New York: Basic Books, 1988). See particularly the introduction and the final chapter on "Criticism Today."

39 Ibid., 229, paraphrasing Breyten Breytenbach.

Three

The Path Marked Out by Charles Davis's Critique of Political Theology

DENNIS P. McCANN

This essay is written from the perspective of one who still struggles existentially with his baptismal inheritance as a Roman Catholic. It is meant to bear witness to what I, and others like me, have learned and continue to learn from Charles Davis. In reading Davis I am struck first of all with an overwhelming sense of his intellectual and spiritual integrity. The uncompromising honesty that I find in his analyses, his capacity for dialogue with those who differ with him, as well as the general direction of his theological reflections in recent years, compel my attention and respect.

My purpose in this essay, however, is not to praise Davis but to understand him better. What follows is a public argument meaning to show but one of the ways in which Davis's life and work has borne fruit for Christian, and especially Catholic, theology. I will try to show the continuity between the concluding part of *A Question of Conscience*, "Prospect for the Church,"[1] and his later work, *Theology and Political Society*.[2] To telegraph my message: Davis recognized that the Church, to be true to itself, must be (or become) a *political* society in the truest sense, that is, a community of moral discourse in which the meaning and purpose of all human endeavour is made explicit and celebrated. For this to happen, of course, the "really existing" Roman Catholic Church would have to be transformed radically. By following up on the leads sketched out in *A Question of Conscience* Davis was later able to challenge us with a political ecclesiology for a universal Church that does not yet exist. If such a Church is ever to be actualized, however, it will be done so along the path marked out by Davis's critique of political theology.

I

A Question of Conscience

It is possible, even in praising *A Question of Conscience*, to misunderstand it. The book is not just Davis's *Apologia pro vita sua*. At issue are more than the vicissitudes of his personal journey toward Christian faithfulness, however instructive others might find such a narrative. The book is an argument about ecclesial structure, the current organizational form of the Roman Catholic Church, and the validity of the policies and practices which this structure characteristically produces. The argument is that of a public person, an Englishman who once had assumed the responsibility of speaking on behalf of that Church, and who finds that in good faith he can do so no longer. Davis, in short, felt he owed us an explanation for what he termed his creative disaffiliation from the Church.

As Davis notes just prior to the opening of "Part III: Prospect for the Church," Rosemary Radford Ruether had rightly characterized his decision as that of "a moderate rather than a radical theologian."[3] The moderation which he previously exercised in defence of the Church now required him to reject the wishful thinking that makes its escape into less than critical forms of theological hermeneutics. Since the really existing Church was not to be placed above suspicion, Davis had to confront its problems, analyze their causes, and spell out what it means to take such an analysis seriously. Vexed by the cumulative evidence that the Church's very structure functioned as an obstacle to growth in faith, hope and love among its members, Davis was forced to expose the nature of the structural fault, and its pathological consequences. His analysis is that the Church's current hierarchical structure is both accidental and a hindrance to the realization of its true mission. The concluding section of *A Question of Conscience* seeks to outline an alternative, the path toward an ecclesiological structure more in keeping with the Church's mission.

"Prospect for the Church" thus opens with "The General Problem," which tries to define the situation of "Christian presence in the modern secular world."[4] This theme, of course, is not a new departure in Davis's theological project, for the problem had already been addressed in his earlier work, *God's Grace in History*. What follows is a Providential reading of "the disappearance of Christendom," that is, the passing of that "single sacred, politico-ecclesiastical order" in which Church and society were regarded as one and the same.[5] Like other theologians welcoming this structural transformation, the most decisive being Harvey Cox's *The Secular City*,[6] Davis distinguishes between secularization and secularism. While secularism is hostile to, and seeks the elimination of the sacred, secularization is "a process of differentiation" in which the autonomy of the secular sphere of "immediate reality" is properly acknowledged over the sacred Mystery that envelops it.

The disappearance of Christendom thus need not mean the eclipse of the sacred, but it does suggest to Davis that the hierarchically constituted "visible Church is not the exclusive area of the sacred nor the community of the exclusively saved."[7] Davis's challenge to the Roman Catholic hierarchy is emphatically Christocentric: "Christianity is an eschatological faith" which cannot be identified with any particular culture; moreover, the culture that sustains hierarchy, in light of a historical understanding of the processes of secularization, must be regarded as essentially a residue of "paganism."[8] The Christendom that emerged partially accommodated to this paganism obscured the fact that "the biblical God is not a supporter of the status quo, but a God who breaks it up." Confessing this eschatological faith means that Christians must regard the Church in a new way: "Rather than being a settled nation, with a fixed hierarchical structure, the Church is a pilgrim, nomadic people, constantly uprooted, constantly on the move, needing constantly to improvise to meet new and unexpected situations."[9]

It is Davis's contention that theologians, notably those of his Roman Catholic colleagues most committed to the spirit of Vatican II, have blunted the force of this eschatological faith by falling for the seductive beauty of idealizing abstractions. In order to waken his fellow Roman Catholics from their dogmatic slumbers, Davis proposes to move in precisely the opposite direction: "I am concerned with an acceptance of modern consciousness sufficiently firm and coherent to bring about a change in the structure of the Church as a social entity."[10] In order to provoke this change, or at least defend its reasonableness, Davis must next sharpen his readers' awareness of "The Change in Man's Self-Understanding." If secularization is a process that tends toward accepting the proper autonomy of the secular realm, what was the status quo from which it emerged?

Davis sees the change in humanity's self-understanding in terms of a series of polarities. The most crucial involves "a shift from a concept of a fixed human nature to that of a person in the process of becoming himself in freedom."[11] This contrast is generally recognized and celebrated as the anthropological paradigm shift operative in the mainstream of theological response to Vatican II.[12] But here too, Davis goes beyond most of his former colleagues, observing that such a heightened awareness of the scope of human freedom must put believers on a collision course with any cosmically grounded principle of hierarchy. With understandable enthusiasm, Davis celebrates modernity as "the discovery of the person as a freely self-constituting or self-creative conscious subject."[13] He distinguishes between "essential freedom" and "effective freedom," noting that while the former is the presupposition of the latter, it is the latter that is at issue in the critical questions which he must ask about the hierarchical structure of the Church.

Davis insists, however, that both aspects of human freedom entail the recognition of limits. The exercise of "the dynamic structure found in man enabling him to make free decisions," essential freedom, is contingent upon the realization of effective freedom which, in turn, is conditioned in both its "interior" and "exterior" dimensions. Critical reflection suggests that any social structure may play either an enabling or an inhibiting role with reference to effective freedom. The exercise of authority within religious organizations, in particular, is not to be dismissed, for Davis recognizes among the conditions of effective freedom an "authority understood as a creative and formative truthful guidance at the service of freedom both individual and social and adapted to the actual needs of men."[14]

Hardly antinomian in its intent, Davis's conservative view of modern consciousness becomes radical in its practical implications as soon as it is applied consistently to social structures. The third section, "From Hierarchical Orders to Free Organizations," asserts that "the new consciousness is in fact the death warrant for all fixed hierarchical orders."[15] To back this observation up, Davis outlines a flat contrast in theoretical models of social organization: hierarchical structures as such are cosmically grounded, claiming an eternal validity, paternalistic, and closed; whereas the associational structures of modernity are self-consciously historical in origin, hence changeable, tending toward egalitarianism, and open. While hierarchy inevitably tends to demand absolute loyalty and obedience, voluntary association tends to recognize its own limited scope and validity.

Judged against this typology, the voluntary forms of association typical of modernity must be regarded as a "liberation" from the "imposed and preformed relationships" characteristic of hierarchical orders.[16]

Nevertheless, Davis remains cautious about the prospects of modernity. Since all forms of social organization carry with them their own unique disadvantages, the limited capacities of voluntary association to achieve human fulfillment must also be recognized. Following Harvey Cox, Davis focuses on the significance of "I-You" relationships that are reducible to neither of the poles offered by Martin Buber's analysis in *I and Thou*. Thus, Davis is not about to condemn the formation of modern bureaucracies so long as they recognize the limits of their legitimately administrative functions; nor is he taken aback by the predictable failure of voluntary associations to realize the nostalgic ideals of *Gemeinschaft*. Social organizations, including the Churches, must resist the temptation to return to the archaic world of hierarchy simply because it may have been cozier.

The social costs of modernity, however, are not insignificant. "The open situation in which men are now placed has created the modern problem of loneliness."[17] Furthermore, the pervasive but limited character of "I-You" relationships may exacerbate the problems of marginalization faced by groups "deprived of reasonable social opportunities and unable to share fully in social life." But the solution to these problems is not some totalitarian pursuit of a "single, over-arching organization," a recrudescence of Christendom or even more narrowly based loyalties, but "the creation and development of a common world of meaning . . . [acknowledging] a universal human fellowship."[18] Here Davis anticipates later theological discussions of the meaning of religious and cultural pluralism, and courageously refuses the tribalization of moral and religious discourse that seems to have sidetracked his more self-consciously radical colleagues.

While Davis's reflections on the existential problem of living with modernity are important here for understanding his later work, his focus remains riveted to the question of the Church. While "the social structure of the Church has not been unaffected by modern organizational society," it has absorbed these developments to form itself "into a vast administrative structure, endeavouring to control, arrange, and systematize the activity of Christians."[19] By refusing the application of the principles of modernity to itself, it has created a structure that "shows the worst, inhuman, bureaucratic features of modern organizational society without allowing and fostering its advantages." Assisted by modern organizational technology, "the Church is crushing the humanity of Christians and frustrating their personal and social expansion as Christians."[20]

The next section, "The Historical Approach to Truth and Faith," makes explicit the epistemological basis not only of Davis's critical ecclesiology but also of his hope for universal human fellowship beyond the wreckage of Christendom. Here, too, the thrust of Davis's remarks is moderate, but with socially radical implications. His epistemological theory, no doubt inspired by Bernard Lonergan's *Insight: A Study of Human Understanding*,[21] is actually closer to Charles Sanders Peirce's "contrite fallibilism":[22] "Man's relation to truth is that of unceasing pursuit in the context of open questioning."[23] Such questioning, however, "can never entirely prescind from or escape the limited perspectives imposed upon . . . [human enquirers] as subjects involved in an historical process." Nevertheless, a partial transcendence is possible to the extent that, by endless questioning, a person "can approximate his knowledge ever more closely to objective reality and avoid imprisonment in any particular subjective standpoint or historical perspective."[24] Though Davis is quick to point out its skeptical implications relative to the untenable claims of nonhistorical orthodoxies, it is also clear that this fallibilism maintains its objectivity by appealing to the systematic exercise of cognitive rationality within a community of enquiry. The perspectival limitations of individual enquirers can be overcome, to some extent, through the institutionalization of genuinely open forums of public discourse.

Like Peirce, and others who have explored the social nature of cognitive rationality, Davis is impressed by the success of "the scientific community" in establishing such processes of open communication.[25] But instead of exploring further the nature of such processes, Davis underscores their ecclesiological implications. The most important is that the social nature of cognitive rationality renders a juridically enforceable Magisterium superfluous. Not only is the idea of orthodoxy, as an unhistorical absolute, epistemologically unwarranted, but also counterproductive with reference to the religious concerns that animate its defenders.

Granted, the integrity of Christian faith as "a personal commitment to God through Christ" does rest upon the continuity of historical tradition. But such continuity cannot be safeguarded by promoting the illusion of "a total God's eye-view of Christ, unconditioned by any particular standpoint or historical perspective," but may be approximated by subordinating "all the limited, perfectible formulations to the preservation of Christian commitment in a succession of different cultures and to the drive toward a better understanding of Christ and his work, and . . . [by verifying] the fact that no development leads to the dissolution of that commitment."[26] If the continuity of Christian tradition is to be cultivated, the Church must become an open community of enquiry:

> These conditions, I am convinced, will be realized only by regarding Christian truth as belonging to the Christian community as a whole, as in fact being the common world of meaning that constitutes it as a community. . . . Open communication will secure that relevant questions are not suppressed, but are taken up by others and met by common effort. Through it the inadequacy of particular formulations will be revealed and counteracted by fresh thought to meet new situations and problems. Open communication can provide the remedy for errors.[27]

Davis thus agrees with Hans Küng's later distinction between the indefectibility of the Church and the alleged infallibility of the Magisterium.[28] Though the claim of infallibility is clearly incompatible with a fallibilist epistemology, Davis still affirms "the promised support and guidance of the Spirit" in the ordinary workings of the processes of open enquiry: "As long as there remains a sufficient hold upon Christian truth by Christians to form the basis for a renewal and eventual opposition to any error, the continuity of Christian tradition is safeguarded."

If the Magisterium is thus rendered superfluous, and Christian faithfulness is not to be subject to administrative regulation, what is the purpose of "the visible Church"? Davis pursues this question in the following section on "The Christian Church and the Wider Society." His answer clarifies the Church's indispensable role in achieving universal human fellowship: "The visible Church is the disclosure of what is present universally in human life and history. It stands as the permanent embodiment of the explicit revelation of God's purpose for all mankind."[29] Such a definition fits well within the mainstream of ecclesiological thought articulated at Vatican II, but Davis's perspective focuses on the manner of that disclosure, whose significance is given in Christian fellowship:

> The Christian life is the strengthening, promotion and celebration of all good and genuinely human life. It is not the creation of a special kind of existence nor the erection of a separate form of religious life nor the following of an exclusively Christian way of life.

Christian fellowship is the discovery and building up of universal
human fellowship . . . the manifest emergence of that common world
of meaning which is constitutive of the human community itself.[30]

Consistent with his earlier appreciation of secularization, Davis thus
insists that the boundary between Church and society is and must remain
fluid. Since the visible Church is not to be regarded as "the exclusive area of
the sacred," there is no point in creating "a single over-arching organization"
representative of the totality of Christian mission. In this vein, Davis
emphatically rejects what was then the conventional goal of Christian
ecumenism, the reunion of all ecclesial bodies in "one vast, unified
organization."[31] Any such move would inevitably tend to preserve an
outmoded and idolatrous hierarchical order that has proven to be a great
obstacle to the free exercise of Christian mission.

So Davis rejects the ecclesiological alternatives represented by Ernst
Troeltsch's typology of "societal Church" and "sect."[32] Neither is adequate
as a norm for ecclesial development, because both fundamentally distort the
nature of the Christian community's mission in history which is to render
visible and explicit the "universal human fellowship" that God is building in
the world. How Davis can regard such a mission as feasible apart from a
juridically formalized structure is testimony to the depth of his faith in the
integrity of Christian tradition. Christians, in his view, participate in a
common culture whose distinctive signs apparently cannot be disfigured
beyond recognition, anymore than God's Grace can ultimately be defeated.
The visible Church, at any given moment of its history, is sufficiently
capable of revealing these signs, but none of its manifestations is absolutely
necessary. Church officials therefore have no reason to assert their own
indispensability. God's Grace being what it is in history, the work of creating
the universal human fellowship, can go on as easily without them as with
them and perhaps more so.

Davis's critique reaches its most provocative point in the next section on
"The Sacraments." What he says there is merely a logical extension of the
argument that he has outlined in the previous sections, but here it is directed
very tellingly to the concerns of Roman Catholics, like myself, who share
virtually all of Davis's convictions but hesitate to draw the practical
conclusion that he has made. Such is the problem of those who, "despite all
doubts and difficulties, stay within the Roman Catholic Church because they
cannot relinquish the sacraments, especially the Mass."[33] Davis refuses to

judge such persons; indeed, he insists that they must follow their consciences: "What is important is that people should cling to Christ according to their present understanding." But he must offer an explanation for following a different path which at the very least has logic on its side.

Davis shares with his former colleagues the conviction that "the visible Church is the fundamental sacrament in so far as it is the permanent, manifest presence of Christ in the world, the visible expression and embodiment of his union with men, the effectual sign of his saving gifts."[34] But this affirmation implies for him a decisive negation: " . . . the seven sacraments, including the Eucharist, could not themselves be regarded as fundamental." Consequently, the hierarchical structure of the Roman Catholic Church cannot be justified by appealing to current sacramental practices: "Since the seven sacraments are actions of the Church, their structure is determined by the structure of the Church."

> The general structure of the Church as a community must first be determined and then it will be possible to see how that community will express its Christian faith and commitment in its chief and distinctive actions, namely the sacraments.[35]

If there is a "Gordian knot" to be untied on the way to reforming the Roman Catholic Church, surely Davis has severed it. The traditional norm of Christian orthopraxis, *Lex orandi, lex credendi*, here stands exposed in its paralyzing ambiguity. The sacramental practice of the Church itself ought to reflect the truth of Christian faith, and not be allowed to determine unilaterally the valid range of meanings implicit in that truth. Its unhistorical orthodoxy is rendered untenable in principle by Davis's fallibilism, as is any uncritical appeal to orthopraxis. Roman Catholics should not allow their understandable reverence for the Church's sacraments to become an obstacle to, or an apriori definition of, the limits of structural change.

In the final section, then, Davis offers a clarification of his policy of "Creative Disaffiliation." The practical consequences of his critical ecclesiology can be evaded only by escaping into "an unreal world" of theological abstraction. Though his colleagues may find such a retreat expedient, Davis is convinced that Christian faith compels another response:

> Institutions and social structures have meaning. The Christian faith as it exists in concrete fact is not to be found primarily in what

theologians write about it, but in the meaning embodied in the
structures and institutions of the Church and in the relationships,
attitudes and actions these give rise to. If the social structures of the
Church no longer embody a valid meaning, the Church is presenting
and living a corrupted and distorted faith.[36]

Creative disaffiliation, however, is a posture that seeks to address this
problem, not by simply removing oneself discretely from the source of the
corruption, but by creating a space external to the institution from which
effective Christian freedom can be exercised in the cause of reform. For
some, but not all, the struggle will involve formal "renunciation of their
denominational membership." Though Davis felt forced to take this step
himself, he's clearly less interested in defending this as the only option than
in assisting all faithful Christians to work for the "renewal and
reorganization" of the visible Church.

II

Theology and Political Society

Unlike *A Question of Conscience*, which Davis claims was written with only
minimal reference to other texts, *Theology and Political Society* is a tour de
force of textual criticism. It is for that reason comparatively dense, and its
theoretical rigour clearly is addressed to a different audience, namely, to his
professional peers, Roman Catholic or otherwise. It is also, in my view, the
best book ever written in English in critical response to political theology and
the liberationist perspectives in critical dialogue with it. I remember thinking
when it first came out that this was a book that only Charles Davis could
have written. For few theologians have had their religious praxis critically
tested by life the way Davis's has been. Fewer still have so completely lived
by the maxim of critical enquiry that Kant had dramatized: *Sapere Aude!*

Even so, *Theology and Political Society* first attracted my attention on
the strength of its methodological analysis, the relative superiority of Davis's
critique of the method implicit in political theology, and how he used Jürgen
Habermas's own struggle with Marxist tradition as a model to clarify what
a political theologian must do to make good on the programme of "critical

reflection on praxis." I too had been wrestling with the epistemological breakthrough that this programme represented,[37] and was reassured to discover that Davis had similar concerns about it. But rereading his analysis in light of *A Question of Conscience*, I am struck by the tacit challenge that political theology may have afforded Davis's posture of creative disaffiliation.

Political theologians and the liberationists in critical dialogue with them, on first sight, could hardly be accused of the evasiveness that Davis saw among the mainstream of Vatican II theologians. Political and liberation theologies were focused on questions of secularization, effective freedom, and the validity of inherited social and ecclesial structures. If anything, they were far more explicit in their concerns for the poor and the marginalized than *A Question of Conscience* seems to be. Judged within the Marxist paradigm of social analysis which they were incorporating into their theologies, Davis's understanding of the prospect for the Church must have seemed hopelessly bourgeois in its emphases, and thus as providing unwitting support for the status quo it meant to overcome. Indeed, the solidarity with the oppressed advocated by the new theologies could often be maintained more effectively within the framework of the visible Church than through creative disaffiliation from it. Though Davis never once mentions his earlier work in *Theology and Political Society*, he had to realize that the new theologies, if not developed properly, might divide the cause of ecclesial reform from that of societal transformation. The singular contribution of his later work is to show how the two are, and must remain, completely interdependent.

"From Orthodoxy to Politics," as the first chapter is called, welcomes political theology as a clear advance upon the theology of Vatican II which, in Davis's view, still accepted the primacy of theory over practice: "It was orthodox doctrine interpreted in transcendentalist, existentialist, personalist terms."[38] By contrast, political theology insists on the methodological primacy of praxis over theory which affirms that religious faith, even Christian faith, is always mediated through some cultural element. This insight is an invitation to criticism and active struggle, for if such mediation is inevitable, then faithfulness requires some attempt to become conscious of the inadequacies of inherited cultural forms, and if necessary, to change them. In principle, there are no limits to such criticism; it cannot be restricted by taboos that would regard any given historical embodiment of Christianity as sacred.

The boldness of the new theologies' agenda, however, is rarely matched with equal rigour in execution. The work of Johann Baptist Metz in particular comes under fire for its half-heartedness. Metz offers *"orthopraxis*, not as replacing orthodoxy, but as the price of orthodoxy. . . . The new language covers a traditional outlook."[39] Yet, if the new theologies are be taken seriously, the claim of any institution or group to substantial possession of an orthodoxy is impossible. By the same token, the rhetoric of orthopraxis runs the risk of absolutizing a particular social practice, however socially progressive, as if it were already the ultimate embodiment of the Truth. But Davis's fallibilism, as we have seen, will not countenance such claims: "Permanence and universality in the realm of truth and value . . . [may be] desired achievements; but they cannot be prior claims. Continuity-in-truth, which is the meaning of orthodoxy, is a hoped-for-attainment; it cannot serve as a prior norm."[40]

Despite political theology's inconsistency, Davis is not about to dismiss it out of hand. It has clearly understood the epistemological breakthrough implicit in the critical reflection on praxis, though it has failed to pursue it rigorously. It has also recovered a normative understanding of politics that is focused on the achievement of public consensus regarding ends and values, prior to "the rational adaptation of means to pre-given ends, which is the concern of technical debate among experts or technocrats."[41] And it has affirmed the pursuit of such political ends and values as central to the mission of Christians in society. The remaining chapters of *Theology and Political Society*, therefore, try to reconstruct the programme of political theology in a manner more consistent with its own professed commitment to the primacy of praxis.

"The Acceptance of Modernity," Davis's second chapter, returns to the question that was central to his analysis of the "Prospect for the Church" in *A Question of Conscience*. It also provides a tacit concession that his earlier, more optimistic, view of secularization stands in need of revision, if not the critical implications he drew from it for Roman Catholic ecclesiology. The claim of political theology is to accept modernity and to offer a *theory* of the present modern age. In order to assess the merits of this theory, Davis places political theology in critical juxtaposition to previous efforts to do this, namely, those of Friedrich Gogarten and Harvey Cox, and their earlier work in reflecting on the theological meaning of secularization.

Davis begins his analysis with a recognition of the conflict between modernity and "dogmatic Christianity": "What makes the modern age modern par excellence is its making decisive the actuality of the observable and experimental, in place of a traditional and authoritative past."[42] But in its embrace of modernity, Gogarten's theology of secularization merely "translated the attitudes and values of contemporary society into theological jargon,"[43] which, as we have seen already, is an arbitrary restriction of the emancipatory thrust of critical reflection. Does political theology offer anything better than Gogarten's theory of modernity? Metz, indeed, does recognize the moral ambiguity of modernity and refuses to canonize it, but his manner is frankly reactionary: "Although he takes the Enlightenment as a basic theme, ... he grossly oversimplifies the emergence of modern subjectivity and the history of modern freedoms ... [with] a preunderstanding drawn from Christian faith. He finds in history what he brings to history."[44] So Metz's approach "is hardly one step beyond Bossuet in method, though it exploits a different set of prejudices," a cutting comparison if there ever was one. But an alternative to the quagmire of self-defeating hypercriticism is at hand: Davis is convinced that Jürgen Habermas's critical theory of modernity (which is also a theory of rationality and its emancipatory thrust) is necessary in order to avoid the uncritical excesses of both Gogarten and Metz.

Before proceeding to a more serious theoretical assessment of the neo-Marxist tradition in which Habermas does his thinking, Davis must clarify the practical consequences of political theology's theoretical failure. His third chapter, "Faith and Social Policy," reasserts political theology's good intentions: because modernity elevates the significance of actuality over the claims of an allegedly authoritative past, a critical theology's adequacy to praxis must be determined by its relationship to the processes of societal transformation. All the new theologies accept this critical test in principle, but they are relatively unclear on how to coordinate the experience of faith with the actual vagaries of political action.[45]

It is not surprising that at this point Davis takes up the work of Juan Luis Segundo, far and away the most methodologically rigorous of the Latin American theologians of liberation. Segundo's writings of the relationship of faith and ideology are scrutinized in light of Davis's uncompromising insight into the historical contingency of any social praxis. Segundo, in Davis's view, makes a dichotomy between faith and ideology. Faith is understood primarily in methodological terms as the stimulus for participation in a "deuterolearning process," the content of which is a succession of ideologies which embody commitment to a range of substantive values. As Segundo himself insists, this dichotomy makes it impossible to answer the question of the substantive truth-content of Christian, or any other form of faith.

Davis, of course, remains skeptical of Segundo's dichotomy because of his own fallibilist epistemology which, while repudiating the claims of orthodoxy as such, does find it meaningful to enquire into the substantive continuities of truth within a tradition. He thus compares Segundo's dichotomy with Herbert Richardson's equally dubious distinction between procedural and teleological values. Davis's rejoinder to both underscores the necessity of adjudicating historically contingent truth claims which remain both substantive and methodologically significant: "The procedural values of a *pluralist society*, if they are not just temporary expedients, originate in and continue to imply a set of truths and values concerning the human condition and human destiny."[46] No theologian, therefore, can resolve the problem of mediating faith and political action by retreating to the procedural, or methodological alone, but must engage in a truly critical hermeneutic of traditions and their substantive claims.

Despite Metz's half-heartedness about orthopraxis, Davis returns to his political theology in order to illustrate how such a hermeneutic might proceed, and with what consequences. Once again, the crucial question is raised: "Does the content of Christian faith allow one to derive a political command from it?"[47] Metz answers "No," but he does so for substantive reasons, namely, his "well-known teaching on the eschatological reserve or proviso," in other words, a theological interpretation that places limits on identifying any political programme with the coming Kingdom of God. Metz, of course, still affirms the need for a mediation between faith and political action, but apparently for lack of a better vehicle, he sees it coming not through theology but through ethics.

Davis, in turn, has serious reservations about Metz's position, and they must be examined carefully if they are not to be misunderstood. Davis is firm in his rejection of the role of ethics in mediating between faith and political action: political theology "tries in a nonpolitical fashion to legitimate the political interventions it advocates. By the very fact its political interventions remain politically incoherent, voluntarist and badly opportunist." But this does not constitute a repudiation of political ethics as such. Davis's point concerns the appropriate location of ethical reflection within the overall process of Christian social action. Ethics is no substitute for a genuine practical theology:

The constant appeal to practice in recent theology is just an excuse for a lack of theory. The idea of a spontaneous *orthopraxis* is a myth.

Recourse is had to ethical inspiration to cover over the absence of theoretical criteria for action. But where there is a situation of oppression, a practice inspired by an ethics of change comes both too early and too late. Too early: because it comes without the work of analysis necessary to make it adequate and effectual in dealing with the oppression. Too late: because theory is thereby led to constitute itself in relation to ethical rather than political practice and is not therefore, as it should be, a theoretical discourse arising out of a real emancipatory practice.[48]

Make no mistake about this: "The appeal to ethics is an attempt to jump over the gap left empty by the absence of social theory."[49] The social theory that could mediate between Christian faith and political action would be, in the first place, a political ecclesiology capable of confronting honestly "the lack of any real and effective functional relationship between Christian institutions and society as at present organized."[50] But such an ecclesiology Davis had already outlined in the concluding section of *A Question of Conscience*, which provided a preliminary sketch of an organizational theory for Christian institutions in a modern society. As Davis pointed out both then and now, the failure of theologians, Roman Catholics especially, to develop such a theory is directly attributable to the impasse over religious praxis within the Church which, in turn, is a reflection of the Church's moribund social structure.

The consequences of this failure are not just theoretical. They make it impossible for any truly emancipatory social praxis to emerge under Church auspices, despite the good intentions of political theologians and their liberationist allies:

Christian talk on politics has become unreal, stripped of both theory and programme, because it is the free-ranging speech of the disengaged. This is not to deny the personal commitment of Christian individuals and groups. But that commitment remains an essentially private affair. The Christian communities as organized communities stay uncommitted in practice, even though hortatory generalities upon social matters circulate among their members. . . . Meanwhile, the Christian people accept a political pluralism within their Christian communities of a kind that effectively neutralizes any political significance the Christian faith might have. Political theology has not succeeded in counteracting that neutralization, because it continues to reify the Christian tradition and interpret the transcendent quality of faith in an unreal and abstract fashion.[51]

Anyone who has struggled, like myself, to mobilize the Roman Catholic Church to implement its vaunted social teaching more effectively, or who has puzzled over the way in which political divisions within each Christian denomination in North America roughly parallel those of society as a whole, must concede the plausibility of Davis's analysis.

The pastoral letter process of the National Conference of Catholic Bishops in the United States, far from refuting Davis's observations, seems to confirm them. The process of open dialogue, and the critical participation of laypersons in it, held out the promise of becoming a model for the "broadly based, pluralistic, democratically functioning and critically conscious public opinion within the Church" that Davis foresees as the key to developing "a consensus in regard to political policy and action." But that process has foundered precisely when it was used to address issues, such as the role of women in the Church, that are themselves a direct reflection of the impasse regarding the transformation of the Church's own social structure. Davis's analysis, if I read him correctly, is not meant to foreclose the kind of pluralism based on differences in "prudential judgment" that even the pastoral letters wished to legitimate. But it does help account for the way discussions of Catholic social teaching tend to generate their own characteristic forms of ideological distortion, based ultimately not on overt political differences but on the tacit acquiescence by all parties in "an inadequate model of the Christian community." Davis comments:

> In the nature of the case there will be differences, necessitating compromise and mutual tolerance, but it is not too much to suppose that a public opinion formed among Christians in a discussion free from domination and constraints would reach sufficient agreement on key issues for effective participation in emancipatory political policy and action.[52]

The ironies involved in Davis's choice of a neo-Marxist critic as a conversation partner for an enquiry focused on "Freedom of Discourse and the Authority of Tradition," can scarcely be exhausted as a stimulus to critical reflection. Still, Habermas is an obvious candidate, and must be regarded as a kindred spirit, especially by Roman Catholic theologians whom experience has taught to regard the workings of the Holy See as uncannily similar, in aims if not always in methods, with those of the "really existing socialism" of the former Soviet bloc. Like Davis, Habermas was forced to accept a "creative disaffiliation" from the community of faith that nurtured him, long before the "Annus mirabilis" of 1989. Indeed, the Frankfurt School that developed the neo-Marxist critical theory of society was clearly opposed in principle to both the orthodoxy and orthopraxis of Marxist-Leninism from the very beginning. Thus Davis, now pursuing the outlines of a similar theory of the role of Christian institutions in a modern, secularized society, must ask Habermas: if political theology is stalled in a flight from political reality, are there theoretical resources to help pull it out of its eschatological spin?

Habermas's critical theory of society, because it has managed to stabilize a moment of *internal* resistance within the tradition of Marxism, is relevant to Davis's attempt to construct a valid political ecclesiology. The challenge addressed by Habermas in Marxism is remarkably similar to that faced by Davis with respect to Christianity: how to avoid the political irrelevance of sectarianism while not succumbing to the political cynicism of totalitarianism. Parallel to Davis's rejection of both the sect and the societal Church as appropriate forms of Christian community in *A Question of Conscience*, Habermas seeks to define an alternative form of neo-Marxism based on a consensual model of an ideal community of discourse. His theory of communicative action reveals an "ideal speech situation" operative in any attempt to achieve genuine discursivity. The ideal speech situation is normative insofar as a genuine community of discourse simply cannot be established apart from a commitment to open dialogue in pursuit of truth. Habermas's critical theory of society, in short, reaches some of the same conclusions about the nature of human community as Davis already had on the basis of his fallibilist epistemology.

Habermas's theory, nevertheless, falters on the same kind of dichotomy of teleological (substantive) and procedural values that Davis previously rejected in the work of Segundo and Richardson. The community of discourse that Habermas envisions cannot be constituted on formal presuppositions alone, but must embody some sort of moral tradition. (So Davis makes common cause with Hans-Georg Gadamer in his famous dispute with Habermas.) What Davis would like to see from Habermas is some acknowledgement that his own neo-Marxism rests not simply upon the formal characteristics of communicative action as such, but upon the substantive values of the Western liberal tradition. Neo-Marxism can be saved from the distortions of Marxist-Leninist "science" only by recognizing its own dependence upon a moral tradition. Otherwise, the critical theory of society alone is hardly sufficient to become, as Habermas hopes it will, the basis for genuine political community. The praxis of societal transformation, the common cause uniting Habermas and Davis, is impossible apart from a normative tradition. As Davis insists, "Tradition is the author of such transformation, since it is the presence of the Spirit in human history."[53]

This statement, perhaps the most extraordinary and yet logically most indispensable claim in the whole of *Theology and Political Society*, needs discursive validation. Thus the next chapter, "Religion and the Critique of Domination," goes into a deeper dialogue with the Marxist critique of religion. If Davis's invocation of "the presence of the Spirit" is to be affirmed, what has to be true about the nature of social praxis for this claim to be true? Even if Marxism were to revise its self-understanding from a positivistic science to an intellectual tradition sustaining the emancipatory thrust through history, why would it need to recognize the invincible necessity of this religious truth claim? Is the emancipatory project even conceivable historically apart from this faith commitment or something like it?

This question requires Davis to examine critically the Marxist identification of religion with oppression. Again the focus is *theoretical*, because the critique of religion is central to Marx's overall critique of domination and constructive programme for critical reflection on praxis. Since Davis's response to both modernity and the inadequacies of political theology is sharpened through a critical appropriation of the Marxist tradition, he must answer Marx's view of religion in order to warrant his constructive plan for a political ecclesiology.

So Marx's *Theses On Feuerbach* are acknowledged not only for providing the crucial ingredient in the epistemological solvent against orthodoxy formally considered,[54] but also constructively. Since "neither faith nor theology can be considered on its own apart from the development of society in its total reality, . . . a religious tradition (must) not be studied apart from the social group that carries it."[55] But these Marxist appropriations also imply a determinate negation. Unlike Marx, Davis argues that political theology must regard "the critique of religion as belonging to the dynamism of religion itself ": "Religious faith as a thrust toward plenitude and totality, as a pursuit of transcendent truth and value may surely be counted among the sources of emancipatory experience, *and as such,* self-criticism against its own imperfect and corrupt manifestations is built into it."[56] Marx erred, therefore, in failing to see that religious faith was not inevitably an enemy in the struggle against oppression, but actually an indispensable ally. No theologian need apologize for returning the valid insights of Marxism to the communities of faith in which emancipatory experiences may still be nurtured.

If chapter five may be regarded as Davis's critical engagement with Marx and the critique of religion, chapter six, "The Language of Religion and the Language of Politics," is an attempt to adjudicate the same issue with reference to the argument about religion within the neo-Marxist Frankfurt School from which Habermas's own work emerged. Just as authentic religion is an indispensable constituent of any truly emancipatory tradition of criticism, so the language of religion is indispensable to any effective language of politics. The question is reformulated as a question of language because that is what the debate about religion with the Frankfurt School, like most forms of twentieth century philosophy, has been about.

Davis thus revisits the agnosticism of Habermas's mentors Max Horkheimer and Theodor W. Adorno and concedes, as any sympathetic reader must, the "Stoic dignity in the melancholic attitude" that their reflections convey. Nevertheless, Davis insists that such a perspective is "unstable" if the point of it is to sustain a community engaged in the praxis of societal transformation. Habermas, by contrast, is far more straightforward. Curiously similar in his views to those of hardline positivists within the British tradition of analytic philosophy, Habermas insists that "post-metaphysical thought no longer disputes individual theological assertions, but declares the meaninglessness of all theological statements."[57] Undeterred, Davis follows the German theologian, Helmut Peukert, in developing an immanent critique of Habermas's position.

The death of our conversation partner(s) calls into question the meaningfulness of any community of discourse (*Kommunikationsgemein-schaft*), based exclusively on the formal characteristics of communicative action as such. To be committed, as Habermas is, to the project of creating such a community of discourse, one is driven to make an act of faith in "a reality that saves from death":

Death destroys the solidarity created by communicative action, on which we depend for our identity and growth. To affirm communicative action as an irreducible and indispensable element of human existence without evading the fact of death or falling into self-contradiction is to affirm the presence of a reality that saves from death and thus discloses itself in human solidarity. In brief, it is to affirm God as the Judeo-Christian tradition presents him.[58]

Confronted with the *aporia*s of death, the claims of religious language deserve a second hearing. And so, Walter Benjamin, Metz, and especially the insights into religious narrative offered by Flannery O'Connor, Paul Ricoeur, and John Dominic Crossan, are invoked to show the promise of religious language. Yet this promise is also inescapably political in its reference to the praxis of societal transformation: "The merely factual, even when understood supernaturally, is the destruction of every genuine religious meaning. Openness to the transcendent becomes on the level of human experience openness to the future and its unformulable possibilities."[59] But this is precisely what politics is all about—the pursuit of human ends in common.

Davis's final chapter, "Pluralism, Privacy, and the Interior Self," provides a demonstration of what a critical theology is prepared to contribute to an emancipatory politics. It is unlike anything I'd ever seen up to that point in the literature of political and liberation theology. It is also the most explicit point of convergence and yet advance upon *A Question of Conscience*. Davis begins by reasserting the claims of an ultimately religious interiority beyond the empty reality, the "loneliness" as he had previously described it, of modern privacy or bourgeois individualism. This line of argument may seem irrelevant in an essay on political theology, but Davis knows that in order to vindicate his claim for the traditions of biblical faith he must render it plausible with respect to the concrete problem of personal and social development as outlined in the theories offered by neo-Marxism.

The critical test is Habermas's reflections on the "Four States of Social Evolution in Regard to Ego and Group Identity."[60] After reviewing this theory, and highlighting how it predictably confirms Habermas's view of the *obsolete* character of explicitly religious forms of socialization, Davis recapitulates the *aporia* that had been pointed out, following Peukert, in the previous chapter. The existential question posed by the death of one's conversation partner(s) now becomes the theoretical question of the sustainability of the *cosmopolitan or universal identity* that Habermas sees as the culmination of the evolutionary achievement of a truly "rational society."[61]

Davis, of course, thinks that such a development is—or will be—unsustainable unless its religious roots are explicitly recognized and actively pursued. But to make good on this hypothesis, political theology will have to be transformed in dramatic ways. Envisioning the cosmopolitan or universal identity means broadening the theological horizon to understand and embrace the global reality of religious pluralism. But this expansion is hardly a withdrawal of political theology's commitment to societal transformation. For pluralism, religious or otherwise, is an essential constituent of politics; or else, there are no significant differences regarding human ends worth discussing within the emergent global community of discourse.[62] By the same token, Davis insists that honest ecumenical conversation at the global level will remain barren without a transformation of social structures, beginning with the Church and the meaning of Church membership.

Latent in these remarks, I believe, is a telling clarification of the constructive *mission* of those who are forced into some form of creative disaffiliation from the existing Churches: those so engaged are to assist in the birth of a "universalistic structure of religious identity" that is, or will be, "a new articulation, beyond particularism and orthodoxy, of the religious identity of the past, *not its abolition without remainder*." Being forced to stand on the periphery of a Church that falsely, or at least prematurely, identifies itself with this universal religious identity, may constitute a unique opportunity for effective participation in the emerging global ecumenism. Creative disaffiliation need not result in self-marginalization if its focus can be shifted from the disruptions of an increasingly dim past to the promise of future collaborations. A genuinely political ecclesiology must envision a future toward which its social praxis is oriented.

Consistent with the understanding of faithfulness as an aspiration toward historical continuity as outlined in *A Question of Conscience*, Davis tries one last time to synthesize Habermas's formalism with a substantive theological question in order to explain how such continuity toward an emerging universal religious identity might be pursued:

> Participation in communication processes for the formation of norms and values *is a basis* for a universalistic ego-structure, transcending the particularism of enclosed groups. But such a universalistic ego-structure does not of itself imply the unconditional worth of the individual. Are we then simply to relinquish the Christian stress upon the individual self? After all, the doctrine of an individual self, distinct from God, but

constituted in relationship to him, is *not* shared by the nontheistic religious traditions.[63]

Davis's answer is to suggest that Christians, even creatively disaffiliated Christians, would come to the table for dialogue with this gift in hand. The point would not be to impose such a Christian affirmation upon a recalcitrant world (as the defenders of orthodoxy might do), but to put it in play—in a new, globally ecumenical discourse—as a perspective that makes redeemable truth claims at a universal level.

Political theology, Davis implies in conclusion, is best poised to enter into the global dialogue at this point. Its critique of the privatization of religion, properly understood, should be cherished as a brief on behalf of the Christian tradition of interiority. Within Western civilization, at least, no humane politics of societal transformation are possible apart from a recognition of that tradition's legitimate claims.

III

Conclusion

Enough has been said to suggest that Davis's own test of faithfulness, namely the pursuit of *continuity* within a historical tradition, has been demonstrated in his critique of political theology and his sketch for its reconstruction. *Theology and Political Society* decisively advances our theoretical understanding of the political ecclesiology that Davis had already outlined in the "Prospect for the Church" which concluded *A Question of Conscience*. Here are four points, by way of summary, in which the work of the later Davis fulfills the promise implicit in that of the earlier Davis:

(1) In retrospect, Davis was doing *critical reflection on praxis* before there was a methodological vocabulary to define this approach. His resolute attention to the realities of Catholic practice and its structural features forced him to critical reflection. Critique was never an evasion of the demands of social praxis, but forced him to shift the social location from which those demands could be met, at least insofar as his personal situation was concerned.

(2) The fallibilist epistemology that Davis outlined in the chapter on "Truth and Faith" in *A Question of Conscience* essentially anticipates his reception of the Marxist "epistemological breakthrough," that is, not only the primacy of praxis but also its essentially historical character in *Theology and Political Society*. For Davis, the correct inference from this breakthrough is *the end of orthodoxy* not as a fact, but certainly as an intellectually responsible position, and by the same token, *no future for orthopraxis* if that term means any absolutization of the Church's current structures and policies, including the Roman Catholic Church's seven sacraments. In spelling out a critical alternative to orthodoxy and orthopraxis, Davis's epistemological appeal to Marxism here is no fad. It does not signal a loss of either faith or reason. The Marxist insight still remains, even after the collapse of "really existing socialism," the most pointed formulation of the consequences of any genuine thinker's struggle toward critical realism. Theologians, such as myself, who have always been skeptical of Marxist politics, still can learn from this insight.

(3) Davis's understanding of modern society and the Church's role in it is considerably sharpened by his appropriation of critical social theory. But the continuity is equally obvious. A dialectical interpretation of modernity allows us to resist the temptation to celebrate the Enlightenment uncritically, as if its promise of universal freedom or emancipation from oppression were already realized. Experience suggests that things are more complicated than that. Thus the *undialectical* contrast of modern and hierarchical forms of organization outlined in *A Question of Conscience*, for example, needs to be criticized for its oversimplification as the general thrust of Davis's *Theology and Political Society* suggests. The hierarchical model has been transformed in modern forms of social organization, for example, business corporations and non-profit organizations, including universities, but it has not been eliminated. Davis's original sketch threatens to shatter into the fragments of a self-defeating utopianism.

This threat is removed with an assist from Habermas as Davis goes beyond the contrasting models to appropriate critically the ideal of a community of discourse as a formal norm for judging the validity of any kind of social organization. Modern democratic societies may be closer to this norm than feudal hierarchies, and again, perhaps not entirely. In any case, Davis allows us to discern the thrust toward emancipation in its concrete relevance for any social and organizational praxis. This too, as Davis's critique of Habermas suggests, is the *ultimate meaning of the Church*. The teleology of freedom, implicit in communicative action, cannot be sustained on formal presuppositions alone. Its real possibility can only be borne by a tradition institutionalized as a community of faith. The struggle to reform/transform the Church is not an evasion of political responsibility. It is the key to any genuinely emancipatory praxis.

(4) But the "really existing" Church, or I should say Churches as Davis does—because the problem is not limited to Roman Catholicism—so far *resists* this interpretation of its emancipatory role in society (or at least resists its organizational implications). Does this disconfirm Davis's analysis? I don't think so, but it does raise the question of where one is to stand while the Church gets its act together. Davis suggests creative disaffiliation in *A Question of Conscience* based on his confidence in the historic momentum of Christianity as a *definable cultural tradition* in Western civilization. In short, creative disaffiliation is not unlike Andrew Greeley's description of the "communal Catholic," though far more principled and nuanced.

With the passage of time, however, one may question both the strength of that momentum and worry about the tendency of creative disaffiliation to become increasingly less creative, increasingly marginal, accompanied by personal feelings of being cast adrift, and an increasingly paralyzing sense of loss and erosion of self-esteem. To be anything more than a personal solution, creative disaffiliation must have a clear and societally transformative purpose. It must be prospective as well as retrospective. What Davis achieves in the final chapter of *Theology and Political Society* is clarity over the global mission of Christians who find themselves marginalized from their own Churches. It may still be lonely out on the periphery but, in light of Davis's insights, being there cannot be dismissed as a meaningless gesture. So we are in Charles Davis's debt. He has marked out a path that marginalized Christians can walk with integrity and faithfulness.

Notes

1   Charles Davis, *A Question of Conscience* (London: Hodder and Stoughton, 1967), 181-241.

2   Charles Davis, *Theology and Political Society* (Cambridge: Cambridge University Press, 1980).

3   Davis, *Question*, 168.

4   Ibid., 181.

5   Ibid., 182.

6   New York: Macmillan, 1965.

7   Davis, *Question*, 185.

8   Ibid., 187.

9   Ibid.

10   Ibid., 190.

11   Ibid., 192.

12   See Charles E. Curran, *Directions in Catholic Social Ethics* (Notre Dame, IN: University of Notre Dame Press, 1985).

13   Davis, *Question*, 194.

14   Ibid., 196.

15   Ibid., 199.

16   Ibid., 201.

17   Ibid., 205.

18   Ibid., 206.

19   Ibid., 208.

20   Ibid., 209.

21   London: Longman, Green, 1958.

22   See Max Fisch, *Peirce, Semeiotic, and Pragmatism*, ed. Kenneth Laine Ketner and Christian J.W. Kloesel (Bloomington, IN: Indiana University Press, 1986).

23   Davis, *Question*, 211.

24   Ibid., 212.

25   Ibid., 216.

26   Ibid., 213.

27   Ibid., 215.

28   See Hans Küng, *Infallible? An Enquiry* (New York: Doubleday, 1971).

29   Davis, *Question*, 211.

30   Ibid., 222.

31   Ibid., 225.

32   Ibid., 227-29.

33   Ibid., 230.

34   Ibid.

35   Ibid., 267.

36   Ibid., 237.

37   See my books, *Christian Realism and Liberation Theology* (Maryknoll, NY: Orbis Books, 1981) and *New Experiments in Democracy: The Challenge for American Catholicism* (Kansas City, MI: Sheed and Ward, 1987). Also see Dennis P. McCann

and Charles R. Strain, *Polity and Praxis: A Program for American Practical Theology* (Lanham, MD: University Press of America, 1990).

38   Davis, *Theology and Political Society*, 2.

39   Ibid., 9.

40   Ibid., 26.

41   Ibid., 21.

42   Ibid., 29.

43   Ibid., 43.

44   Ibid., 48-49.

45   Ibid., 53.

46   Ibid., 57.

47   Ibid., 59.

48   Ibid., 61.

49   Ibid., 64.

50   Ibid.

51   Ibid., 64-65.

52   Ibid., 74.

53   Ibid., 103.

54   Ibid., 130.

55   Ibid.

56   Ibid., 131.

57   Ibid., 140.

58   Ibid., 148.

59   Ibid., 156.

60   Ibid., 159.

61   Ibid., 164.

62   Ibid., 168.

63   Ibid., 174.

Four

Pluralism, Conflict, and the Structure of the Public Good

KENNETH R. MELCHIN

This study unfolds as a dialogue with Charles Davis in *Theology and Political Society*.[1] I begin by introducing two of the central challenges which dynamize Davis's approach to political theology and proceed to discuss how his responses bring him into debate with liberal theory on the meaning of pluralism. In an effort to advance this discussion, I explore some of the contributions from the work of Bernard Lonergan on the structure of social meaning schemes. I argue that Davis's approach involves a rather novel way of conceiving the role of pluralism in political society which can correct some problems in the liberal approach and I draw some critical conclusions for Davis's discussions of theory and praxis. The final section is devoted to advancing Davis's quest for insights into the structure of communicative action which can ground norms for discourse on the public good. While Davis's work draws upon the critical theory of Jürgen Habermas, I draw upon contributions from the field of conflict studies and utilize insights from Lonergan and George Herbert Mead to illustrate the links between structure and norm in social meaning schemes.

The principal conclusions of this study are two. First, Davis is correct in calling for an empirical analysis of the dynamic structure of communicative action to ground norms to regulate a public discourse on the good of political society. Contrary to the supposition of liberal theory, a fully open, fully participatory discourse on the public good is required in order for citizens to nurture and sustain the cooperative social structures which condition their interests and needs. Consequently, the fundamental norms for political society are those that regulate this discourse. Second, the field of conflict studies yields a body of evidence on the potentialities for discourse in situations of conflict which can help advance our understanding of these norms. Bernard Lonergan's concept of "recurrence scheme" provides a useful tool to help refine our understanding of the concrete structures of discourse and for understanding how knowledge of these structures grounds our insight into norms.

I

Universal Rationality and Pluralism: The Challenge of Liberalism

In *Theology and Political Society*, Davis invites us to rethink the social praxis foundations of theology, to rescue theology from its Enlightenment prison of privatized religion, and to transform theology into a fully public, pluralist discourse towards the transformation of political society in favour of the oppressed.[2] While Christian faith has always called for a commitment to "the politics of emancipatory social change,"[3] two obstacles have stood in the way of Christians hearing this call in the modern age. The first of these obstacles has been the Enlightenment, with its liberal heritage of individualism and privatization. Due to the effects of positivism and what Davis calls "the Romantic compromise with positivism,"[4] there emerged in Western societies a distinction between the spheres of the public and the private. The public became the sphere of rational discourse, where rationality was understood in terms of the extant empirical-analytic sciences. In this view, the public realm had to be so restricted because only these sciences could yield grounds for wide-scale public agreement. In contrast, the private sphere of values and religion was understood to be lacking in a rational grounding and, consequently, could only be expected to yield diversity of opinion and feeling. The effect of this wholesale identification of rationality with the empirical-analytic sciences, narrowly defined, was to confine theology and ethics to the private realm of individual living and to prevent Christian faith from performing its transformative role in social and political life.

In Davis's view, the route beyond this heritage of privatized faith involves articulating a wider understanding of rationality and understanding which is grounded in an account of the structure of communicative action. Davis turns to the work of Habermas to find rational norms operative in the structure of human discourse which are universal in their application and which function through the full range of social, political, ethical, and religious living.[5] The failure of the Enlightenment, in his view, was to take extant views of science as the sole standard of rationality. Following

Habermas, Davis looks to an analysis of the structure of communicative action to find norms that operate implicitly in all human discourse situations to govern the ongoing dynamics of communicative action. When these norms are understood and appropriated explicitly in society, they become foundational for a truly universal rationality which can regulate a fully public discourse towards consensus in all spheres of human living.

Davis finds in Habermas's account of the structure of communicative action the grounds for admitting theology into the realm of public, political discourse while preserving the pluralism which an older heritage of authoritative tradition and doctrinal orthodoxy could not tolerate. And it is here, in Davis's call for the fundamental political requirement of valuational pluralism,[6] that we come to the second obstacle which political theology sought to overcome in its commitment to "the politics of emancipatory change," the problem of doctrinal orthodoxy. In the opening chapter of *Theology and Political Society*, Davis defines political theology in opposition to the Roman Catholic doctrinal tradition with its primacy of theory over praxis and its claims to permanence and universality. The Second Vatican Council had succeeded in ending an era of Catholic theology dominated by "Roman classicism."[7] But in maintaining its grounds in a tradition of theoretical orthodoxy, the Council failed to set theology on the road towards significant renewal. For theology to be properly grounded, Davis argues, it must arise out of the social praxis of living faith in diverse cultures and historical ages. To escape from the sterile theoretical orthodoxy of an authoritarian tradition which imposes its categories on disparate cultures, theology must come to recognize a diversity in its doctrine and its institutional forms. To perform its universal task of human liberation, theology must admit a significant pluralism in its knowledge and value claims.[8] It is this standard of theological and ethical pluralism which Davis's concept of universal rationality must uphold and preserve if theology is to be admitted into the sphere of public, political discourse.

However, in insisting upon an irreducible pluralism in theology and ethics, Davis comes face to face with the critique of Enlightenment liberalism which originally had been responsible for banishing theology from political society to the private realm of individuals. While Davis argues that the Enlightenment distinction between the public and private was rooted in a narrow, natural scientific conception of rationality, I would argue that the entire thrust of liberal theory has been to take seriously the requirements of pluralism.[9] The most important of these requirements has been that no religious or ideological system can make a significant claim on the content of public or political life without violating the individual rights and liberties which sustain pluralism. The public sphere is to be reserved only for those principles and procedures of justice which guarantee individual liberties and regulate conflicting claims to individual rights.[10] According to liberal theorists, theology cannot exercise a significant guiding hand in determining "the politics of emancipatory social change" if a serious pluralism is to be ensured. If liberalism is correct, it would seem that we must choose between political theology and pluralism. We cannot have both. As Alasdair MacIntyre points out, liberalism can guarantee a plurality of views of the public good only as long as no view is permitted to shape political society in accordance with the content of its claims.

> Every individual is to be equally free to propose and to live by whatever conception of the good he or she pleases, derived from whatever theory or tradition he or she may adhere to, unless that conception of the good involves reshaping the life of the rest of the community in accordance with it.[11]

I suggest that the criticism which liberal theory raises against political theology requires examining more closely the relation between universal rationality and pluralism. I would argue that in founding his political theology upon the critical theory of Habermas, Davis is appealing to an understanding of pluralism which is significantly different from that of liberal theory. Theorists like John Rawls seek to elaborate theories of justice and rights which will ensure a maximum liberty of individuals which is compatible with similar liberties for all citizens in society.[12] However, they do so without requiring any citizens' participation in shaping the content of the good of public society. Indeed, liberal theory has as its basic presupposition that such participation is neither to be expected nor desired.[13] The overall shape of liberal society is determined by whatever arrangements do not violate minimal, socially contracted standards of equity. The public realm is reserved solely for those principles and institutions which are required to ensure these minimal standards. Within this framework of minimal public limitations, pluralism refers to the rights of citizens to think and to act in accordance with individual interests without regard to the overall shape of the public good. Davis's political theology seems to understand pluralism differently.

There should be a public deliberation about values, through which the implications and consequences of divergent value judgments are comprehensively displayed. The supposition is that open and adequate deliberation will favour the occurrence of correct value judgments on the part of men of good will and thus create a sound public consensus. A pluralist society allows dissent. It does not, however, exclude, but rather as a human society or community of meaning presupposes a consensus, created and maintained freely in open discussion.[14]

Here pluralism refers not to the individual citizen's right to think and act without regard or with minimal regard to the public good, but to a form of his or her participation in a public discourse whose purpose is to determine the content of this public good. Davis's political theology would seem to require the very thing that liberal theory argues to be necessary or impossible: a fully public discourse on the good of political society. Pluralism, far from authorizing or requiring citizens to withdraw from debate on the public good, specifies the form of their participation in this debate. Habermas's theory of communicative action sets the institutional framework and the rules within which this discourse is to proceed. This framework, with its rationally compelling, universal vision of an ideal speech situation, establishes the fundamental agreements with which citizens of diverse views can enter into this discourse.[15] Pluralism, here, is grounded in the mutual recognition among the participants of their respective rights to pursue a discourse towards consensus on truth and value, free from coercion by any force other than the rational force of the argument. This, I suggest, is a radically different understanding of pluralism which cuts to the heart of our understanding of the foundations of a democratic society.

To choose between these competing views of pluralism requires examining the kinds of problems which arise from the structure of social living and which makes demands upon the character of the public good. Social living is constituted by a vast array of complex, concretely functioning structures and institutions of social cooperation which have emerged spontaneously and which can only be regulated or coordinated through wide-scale public input.[16] In the terms of Bernard Lonergan, these structures are "recurrence schemes" which are irreducible structures of meaning and which link together to form wider ecologies of meaning.[17] For the most part, these structures and institutions are cooperative schemes which cannot be controlled or regulated through single decision-making centres, but must be "managed" through the collective efforts of all participants acting with regard to the concerns and values of the other participants in the schemes. As cooperative schemes develop internal structures and link with other schemes which become more and more complex and which make recurrent demands upon their participants, the citizens of society need to understand and choose to act to promote the health of these cooperative structures in order to ensure their survival. Furthermore, because the personal interests and desires which individuals seek to pursue are, in fact, all conditioned by the entire ecology of institutions and meaning schemes in public society, these individual interests can only be attained as long as all citizens participate vigorously to nurture and cultivate the social structures which are essential to their realization.[18]

I would argue that because of the complex, participatory character of the schemes which condition the public good, it is Davis's understanding of pluralism, and not that of liberalism, which must set the grounds for our understanding of democratic liberty. Liberal theory has tended to conceive the public good in terms of an aggregated result of individuals pursuing their interests within the framework of a social contract which authorizes the state to ensure minimal standards of equity in the distribution of liberties. However, this minimal contract will in no way suffice to ensure the adequate form of citizens' participation in the concretely functioning cooperative schemes which condition their living and which make demands upon them in accordance with their internal dynamic structure. For citizens to ensure the good of political society, they must understand and responsibly regulate the full range of cooperative meaning schemes which constitute their living. Moreover, they must do so in dialogue with each other. For in a democratic society, the long range project of political living requires that people from the most diverse, conflicting, and even hostile sectors of society come to understand the respective inputs of all parties into the common schemes which condition the good of all.

The public good is a dynamic ordering which comes to be in the interaction among all the concretely functioning meaning schemes operative in political society.[19] Thus, no single set of abstract principles will suffice to ensure the achievement of this public good. Rather, the road towards the public good requires the long, arduous task of understanding and collectively regulating the concrete structures of meaning which constitute our daily living and which condition the objects of our desires and interests. The fundamental vehicle through which this activity of understanding and collective regulation will go forward is public discourse.

Davis is correct in requiring a fully open, participatory discourse on the public good as the route towards securing the well being of political society. I hold with Davis that pluralism be understood in terms of the apriori norms of openness and respect towards diverse and conflicting views which are necessary to further this discourse towards its goals. However, I would go a step farther than Davis to suggest that this understanding of pluralism also carries implications for the content of the discourse and for the theoretical character of the analysis which the discourse will require. Pluralism, in this view, far from proclaiming all views equally correct, places obligations on the citizens of society to actively seek the refinement and correction of extant views on the public good and to modify individual views in accordance with valid advancements in public knowledge on the good of society. Pluralism implies a set of rights and obligations which will frequently make complex, dialectically related demands of its citizens: first, to respect divergent views; then, to push the discourse forward towards disclosing flaws in these views; and finally, towards the collective enquiry which heads towards mutual discovery.

Furthermore, I suggest that there will be required a level of theoretical differentiation to this discourse on the public good which would seem to call for Davis nuancing his understanding of the relation between theory and praxis.[20] Insofar as any research in theology or in the human sciences makes significant inroads into understanding concrete structures of social meaning, these achievements will yield theoretical insights into the public good which will make demands upon the form of a public praxis which will be truly liberating or emancipatory. To the degree that these insights prove durable, theory will make longer ranging apriori demands upon the social or faith praxis which is to yield the sustained flows of insights that further our understanding of the public good. Certainly, this primacy of theory can in no way be understood as absolute, in the sense that extant theories are conceived to be closed to any or all subsequent revision.[21] However, insights into the normative dynamics of societal structures, if they are correct, will continue to be relevant to societies where these structures are operative regardless of subsequent theoretical developments which set these insights into wider explanatory contexts. In fact, subsequent theoretical developments usually result from and build upon such durable insights. The implication is that these insights will carry the force of a theoretical primacy, both with respect to the praxis which is to live out this vision of the public good and the praxis which will yield further insights into its structure.

II

The Structure of Communication and the Norms of Discourse: Contributions from Conflict Management

To elaborate the theoretical basis for the rational norms which will regulate a theology that is fit to participate in the arena of public discourse, Davis looks to Habermas's theory of "emancipatory interests."[22] Habermas's analysis takes as its point of departure the discovery of three interests which govern or regulate human social action. The first is the technical interest, whose pursuit brings human subjects into discursive action aimed at the coordination of the efforts of members of a social group towards the solving of practical problems. This is the interest governing the realm of human work, the "purposive-rational" realm which calculates means and ends in strategic terms towards the efficient attainment of physical results. The second is the practical interest which brings people into communicative action towards agreement on issues of collective social concern in accordance with consensual norms. This is the interest governing the self-interpretation of society in tradition, society, and culture. The third is the emancipatory interest which functions as a critique of deformations in speech situations of all kinds. The emancipatory interest utilizes political power to redress oppressive constraints that distort communicative action. It functions on a self-reflective level and anticipates an ideal speech situation free from external and internal constraint.

The ideal speech situation anticipated in the emancipatory interest is not ideal in the utopian sense, but is ideal in the sense of an implicit rational norm operative in all communicative action as a tacit expectation of all participants who seek to achieve any concrete objective through rational discourse. The basic thrust of all communicative action, by virtue of its very structure, is to be governed solely by the pursuit of truth, freedom, and justice in emancipated living. Because of the metalevel or self-reflective character of the third, emancipatory interest, it stands apart from the first two, functioning as a higher-order regulatory principle whose goal or object grounds the universal rationality which is intended in all human communication.[23] Consequently, Davis finds in Habermas's analysis the structure of a universal, ideal speech situation which yields criteria for discourse that will be rationally compelling for all humans.

The emancipatory interest requires that participants in discourse appropriate this rational ideal of noncoercive communication as the regulatory norm for their discursive action. Because of the universal character of this interest, Davis can conclude that "norms and values, moral and religious, can be recognized as subject to the procedures and criteria of an intersubjective communication and a prudential or practical rationality."[24] But what requirements or obligations does this emancipatory interest yield? How does this interest give rise to concrete norms or guidelines which will help participants through specific types of discourse situations? I would suggest that to understand how this general ideal of emancipated discourse is to be implemented in political society the analysis needs to be carried further into the empirical and practical study of actual discourse situations. Discourse is a recurrence scheme of interpersonal acts of meaning which has a general structure, but whose concrete characteristics and exigencies only come to light in the course of detailed empirical studies of human experience.[25] Understanding the actual requirements for emancipatory communication requires entering into this empirical enquiry in search of insights into functional and dysfunctional discourse which can be implemented in communicative praxis.

I suggest that the empirical and practical research literature that is currently emerging from the field of conflict studies provides a valuable point of entry into this data base.[26] Conflict researchers study the potentialities for constructive acts of human communication in situations of conflict. Theory and practice from a variety of spheres of human discourse are now beginning to yield insights which pertain both to generic situations of conflict and to field specific realms. Clearly, the limits of this essay permit only a brief introductory overview of what is now proving to be a formidable body of research literature. However, such an overview can help to show how Davis's search for norms governing rational communication in political society can be derived from the empirical study of concrete experiences of functional and dysfunctional discourse, and how this search can be advanced by studying discourse as social meaning schemes.

One of the most influential texts to come out of the major American research centres on conflict is Roger Fisher and William Ury's *Getting to*

Yes: Negotiating Agreement Without Giving In.[27] While the text is presented for a popular audience, it summarizes the achievements of a considerable body of practical and theoretical research in the field and lends itself to introducing some of the broad lines of this research. The book is laid out as a set of norms or guidelines on how to conduct "principled negotiation" towards the settlement of conflicts on the basis of recognizable standards of fairness. While the authors present these guidelines as "negotiation strategies," they are prescriptions or norms whose objective is to guide disputing parties through conflicts towards the achievement of mutually satisfactory goals. My objective in the following discussion will be to show how the authors derive these norms from the structure of discourse in negotiation and how these structures can be understood as social recurrence schemes. The norms appear in the text as ideas or concepts which seem simple and straightforward. However, practitioners in the field recognize that they are extremely difficult to implement regularly with success; they require significant skill development which can take years of practice; and they often require substantial attitudinal changes on the part of disputants who would extricate themselves from dysfunctional habits.[28] As with all norms, these negotiation strategies specify the skills, virtues, and habits which are required for competent or authentic participation in the relevant meaning schemes.[29] The core of the Fisher-Ury text is a set of four imperatives or norms which call for a shift in the disputants' attention from the content of the discourse to its structure and which, if implemented successfully, change the way in which the content is handled by the disputing parties.

> Separate the PEOPLE from the Problem.
> Focus on INTERESTS, Not Positions.
> Invent OPTIONS for Mutual Gain.
> Insist on Using Objective CRITERIA.[30]

These four imperatives arise from the observation that the direction of discourse in situations of conflict is determined not only by the substance of what is being negotiated but also by the procedures for dealing with the substance.[31] These procedures are actually the operative conditions which explicitly or implicitly govern the disputants' movement from speech act to speech act through the negotiation scheme. Conflicts are linked sets of acts of meaning, each act fulfilling the conditions for the next, and the last returning the disputants to some state of satisfaction from which the next discourse scheme can begin. Conflicts often unfold as tempestuous processes, each disputant being battered about by a myriad of forces arising from the proximate or more remote regions of their relationship. However, the four norms invite the disputants to advert to this panoply of forces, to make distinctions among them, and to appropriate action guidelines or objectives correlative with specific characteristics of the structure of the discourse to guide their movement from speech act to speech act through the process.[32]

As the first norm suggests, two kinds of factors or forces that play a significant role in shaping the course of conflicts are those pertaining to the disputants' interpersonal or professional relationship and those pertaining to the problem or issue under discussion.[33] Relationship factors need to be separated from the issue or problem factors. Moreover, contrary to what might be supposed initially, Fisher and Ury argue that it is essential to deal adequately with the relationship issues if negotiation is to proceed successfully. If not, more remote relationship factors rather than those pertaining to the problem will govern the links between the acts of meaning in the discourse. They discuss relationship issues under three headings: perception, emotion, and communication.[34] And it is clear that the central insights throughout each of these discussions involves what George Herbert Mead calls "role taking" or "attitude taking."[35]

One of the first imperatives in dealing with relationships is: "Put yourself in their shoes."[36] In Mead's terms, participants can take the role of the other and see themselves and the relationship from the perspective of the other party, as this perspective is manifested in the other's responses to one's own gestures in the discourse. Discourse proceeds as a linked set of acts of meaning in which participants initiate gestures, make responses to other's gestures on the basis of interpretations of their intended meanings, and engage in subsequent acts of interpretation in which both come to see the other's perception of themselves through the other's responses to their gestures.[37] One of the principal ways in which discourse becomes dysfunctional is through the process of "attribution," wherein participants project upon the other party meanings which escalate conflict and create barriers to communication.[38] Frequently in situations of stress, attributed impressions arise more from one's own fears and stresses than from a careful attention to the other's language and behaviour. Relationship factors can be substantially improved if disputing parties advert to the potential or real differences between the attributed meanings and those which can be gleaned from a more careful attention to the communicative actions of others. In addition, the development of skills and habits of actively listening to verify the intended meanings of others, carefully articulating one's own views in accessible terms, and actively seeking to ensure that one has been correctly understood can substantially increase the capacities of disputants to respond to intended meaning rather than imagined fears.[39]

When the authors move to the second norm, to a discussion of the content issues under dispute, they find a significant structural distinction between two types of content issues: positions and interests.[40] The main insight here is that in many conflict situations, the issues which ground and sustain the dispute are often not the issues which are the explicit focus of the discourse. Behind the explicit positions there often lie interests, concerns, values, fears, and needs which drive the course of the conflict and which need to be discussed and dealt with if the discourse is to achieve mutually acceptable results.[41] Frequently disputants may not even know precisely what underlying interests are driving their own participation in the conflict. Consequently, parties will often need to probe for underlying feelings which will reveal the presence of significant interests.[42] And, most importantly, disputants need to recognize the other's interests as legitimate and give evidence of this recognition, even when they are totally foreign or remote from one's own. It is the mutual recognition and acknowledgement of the respective interests of the conflicting parties which paves the way towards further discourse.[43]

In large measure, the progress of discourse in situations of conflict depends upon the success with which disputants can articulate and clarify the full range of interests which underlie conflicting positions. The reason for this is that solutions to conflict usually require common action strategies, and for action strategies to be common, they need to be built on the basis of common interests. The fascinating feature of communicative discourse in conflicts is that conflicts are driven by a multiplicity of centres, some of which drive the disputants in opposed directions and some of which bring them together in shared concern for common goals. In Lonergan's terms, conflicts are dialectical in structure.[44] It is the shared concerns and interests which bring disputants into conflict in the first place and which keep their diverse interests from resulting in indifference. Understanding this dialectical structure allows disputants to appropriate shared concerns as the basis for dealing with differences. When these shared concerns are identified and mutually recognized, they can become the basis for common action. As a result, the search for "integrative agreements," agreements which are based upon a reconciliation of underlying interests, requires the most dedicated pursuit of common interests even when this pursuit requires probing to the deepest sense of self-worth of the disputing parties.[45]

When the discourse has moved from positions to underlying interests and when progress has been made in identifying common interests, the disputants are ready to move towards implementing the third norm of conflict management: "Invent options for mutual gain."[46] In essence, this norm is based upon an understanding of the structural differences between competitive/win-lose and cooperative/win-win attitudes towards conflict. Its normative thrust is rooted in the growing evidence on the dysfunctional effects of win-lose approaches.[47] Implementing this norm requires appropriating the cooperative approach. However, if the disputants have been successful in recognizing underlying interests and identifying common interests, the search for action strategies will tend somewhat naturally towards cooperative solutions, for the disputants will tend to see each other less as threat and more as partners in a common project.

One of the principal insights behind this norm is that mutually acceptable action strategies are easier to identify when the process of inventing strategies is separated from the process of selection and decision.[48] In Lonergan's terms, understanding and judgment are separate operations which are best performed when participants identify these differences and act accordingly.[49] The main technique for multiplying strategies is "brainstorming," which requires participants to assemble the largest possible array of options and to withhold judgment on all options until the process is completed. While the brainstorming process has the obvious goal of expanding the field of potential action strategies and of increasing the chances of hitting on operable solutions, the process has the added advantage of forcing the disputants to withhold expressing initial "gut reactions" to the other's ideas until a later time when the force of first impressions can be tempered by reflective distance. Finally, brainstorming is itself a cooperative process and the experience of modelling collaboration tends to set disputants on the road towards further cooperation.[50]

The fourth and final imperative, "Insist on Using Objective Criteria," brings the disputants into the process of evaluating and deciding upon common action strategies which will promote their mutual interests.[51] This norm is rooted in the insight that common or objective decision-making criteria will be those which are based on wider, socially accepted standards of action which are implicated in the habitual routines of living of all disputants and which all parties recognize as fundamental for their living. To illustrate this imperative in operation, the authors appeal to a host of examples drawn from the experiences of negotiators in the market place, in international politics, in sports, and in families. The standards which disputants found to be "fair" were those that arose from publicly recognized procedures or schemes for achieving goals or securing services in that realm. The objectivity of the criteria, in each case, was grounded in the mutual recognition of common goals, needs, or objectives which arose in the relevant sphere of living and the common appeal to the public data on extant meaning schemes which have proven their ability to meet these objectives.

While the core of the text is devoted to an elaboration of the four imperatives for principled negotiation, the authors complement this discussion with a response to commonly held objections which arise from experiences of unfair practices, the utilization of power tactics, or the use of "dirty tricks" in the bargaining.[52] In these chapters, as in the others, the text is chock-full of concrete norms or guidelines for reversing imbalances of power, for disarming opponents who use unfair tactics, and for "Taming the Hard Bargainer."[53] Clearly these guidelines are rooted in general norms of cooperation and fairness which derive from apriori structures of communication. However, the concrete character of each guideline and each negotiation technique arises from the authors' attention to the specific structure of typically recurring schemes of discourse in specific types of situations. Moreover, the normative force of each imperative or "negotiation strategy" is rooted in the proven evidence of its ability to achieve its objectives in the specified discourse scheme. It is the authors' empirical attention to the specifics of these meaning schemes which yields the panoply of concrete insights that ground the norms.

Clearly, the overview represents a very brief introduction to a massive field. The discussion could continue to engage research and practical results on third party interventions, on the structural features associated with multiparty and community conflicts, on the distinctive characteristics of family mediation, international negotiation, mediation education, environmental conflicts, and terrorist negotiations. In each case, researchers, attentive to the specifics of human experience, have hit upon insights into the distinctive structural characteristics of concrete discourse schemes in that realm; they have discerned goals which are correlative to structural dynamics of these schemes; and they have elaborated norms or prescriptions for regulating the schemes toward these goals. I would suggest that the continued analysis of the links between empirical knowledge of social meaning schemes and the norms which regulate discourse in these schemes would continue to advance and build upon Davis's search for the conditions for emancipatory discourse. Davis has conceived his project as a search for rational norms which would regulate theology's input into this public discourse. However, further enquiry may well reveal that in addition to finding norms to govern its entry into the public sphere, theology may have its own contribution to make towards understanding these norms.[54]

III

Conclusion

I have sought to show how insights from the works of Lonergan, Mead, and from the study of conflict can advance Charles Davis's understanding of the conditions for a fully participatory discourse on the good of political society. Social living is constituted by a vast ecology of cooperative meaning schemes in which individuals coordinate their living in accordance with a perceived order in the inputs of all other participants in the schemes. For the most part, the meaning schemes which constitute social life cannot be managed from single decision-making centres but must be regulated through the cooperative efforts of all partners in the relevant schemes. To the extent that social meaning schemes become complex, their internal structures and their links with other schemes need to be understood by the participants if they are to be regulated adequately. The principal route towards this collective activity of understanding is public discourse. Consequently, the fundamental norms for regulating political society will be those derived from an analysis of the normative dynamics of discourse.

This understanding of social living gives rise to a distinctive understanding of pluralism. Far from granting citizens a right to any and all views, pluralism specifies the form of their participation in a public discourse whose aim is to understand the social schemes which make demands upon their participation in the public good. Davis looks to Habermas to understand the general structure of discourse and for general norms of discourse which arise from this understanding. The field of conflict theory advances this understanding of the concrete potentialities and skills required for discourse in situations of conflict. Finally, when structures of discourse in conflict are understood as social recurrence schemes, the links between structure and norm become clearer.

Notes

1   Charles Davis, *Theology and Political Society* (Cambridge: Cambridge University Press, 1980).

2   Ibid., 175-78.

3   Ibid., 51.

4   Ibid., 177.

5   Ibid., 75-97, 169, 177-78.

6   Ibid., 167-69.

7   Ibid., 1.

8   Ibid., 1-26, especially 1-4, 26, and 167-69.

9   John Rawls, *A Theory of Justice* (Cambridge, MA: Harvard University Press, 1971), 13-14, 144; Alan Gewirth, *Human Rights* (Chicago: University of Chicago Press, 1982), 4-7; and Alasdair MacIntyre, *Whose Justice? Which Rationality?* (Notre Dame, IN: University of Notre Dame Press, 1988), 335-38.

10   MacIntyre, *Whose Justice? Which Rationality?*, 335-38.

11   Ibid., 336.

12   Rawls, *A Theory of Justice*, 14-15, 60-65.

13   Ibid., 12, 13-14, 57, 142-45.

14   Charles Davis, "The Philosophical Foundations of Pluralism," in I. Beaubien, Charles Davis, Gilles Langevin, eds., *Le pluralisme: Symposium interdisciplinaire/Pluralism: Its Meaning Today* (Montreal: Fides, 1974), 247; cited in *Theology and Political Society*, 168-69.

15   Davis, *Theology and Political Society*, 79-97, 168-69.

16   See Kenneth R. Melchin, "Moral Knowledge and the Structure of Cooperative Living," *Theological Studies* 52 (Fall 1991): 495-523; and Patrick Byrne, "Jane Jacobs and the Common Good," in Fred Lawrence, ed., *Ethics in Making a Living* (Atlanta, GA: Scholars Press, 1989), 169-89.

17   Bernard Lonergan introduces the concept of the "recurrence scheme" in *Insight* (New York: Philosophical Library, 1958), 118-20. "The notion of the scheme of recurrence arose when it was noted that the diverging series of positive conditions for an event might coil around in a circle. In that case, a series of events, A, B, C, . . . would be so related that the fulfillment of the conditions for each would be the occurrence of the others. Schematically, then, the scheme might be represented by the series of conditionals: If A occurs, B will occur; if B occurs, C will occur; if C occurs, . . . A will recur. Such a circular arrangement may involve any number of terms, the possibility of alternative routes, and in general, any degree of complexity" (118). Also

see Philip McShane, *Randomness, Statistics and Emergence* (Dublin: Gill and Macmillan, 1970), 206-29.

18   On the conditioning links between individual desires or interests and social recurrence schemes, see Melchin, "Moral Knowledge and the Structure of Cooperative Living."

19   Patrick Byrne distinguishes a static, "common good" approach from a dynamic, historically conscious approach towards understanding the public good in "Jane Jacobs and the Common Good."

20   See Davis, *Theology and Political Society*, 2-4, 26, 89-90, 101-103.

21   Ibid., 26, 178. This concern, that theology be understood as continually open to revision, is clearly important for Davis.

22   Ibid., 80-97.

23   Ibid., 88-89.

24   Ibid., 178.

25   See Melchin, "Moral Knowledge and the Structure of Cooperative Living." Also see Melchin, *History, Ethics, and Emergent Probability* (Lanham, MD: University Press of America, 1987), 185.

26   Recent texts which introduce the breadth and depth of the field include Susan Carpenter and W.J.D. Kennedy, *Managing Public Disputes* (San Francisco: Jossey-Bass, 1988); Roger Fisher and Scott Brown, *Getting Together* (Harmondsworth: Penguin, 1989); Roger Fisher and William Ury, *Getting to Yes* (Harmondsworth: Penguin, 1983); Victor Kremenyuk, ed., *International Negotiation* (San Francisco: Jossey-Bass, 1991); Kenneth Kressel, Dean Pruitt, and Associates, *Mediation Research* (San Francisco: Jossey-Bass, 1989); Christopher Moore, *The Mediation Process* (San Francisco: Jossey-Bass, 1987); M. Afzalur Rahim, ed., *Managing Conflict* (New York: Praeger, 1989); Howard Raiffa, *The Art and Science of Negotiation* (Cambridge, MA: Harvard University Press, 1982); and Dennis Sandole and Ingrid Sandole-Staroste, eds., *Conflict Management and Problem Solving* (New York: New York University Press, 1987).

27   Lawrence Gaughan introduces *Getting to Yes* as a text which "may be, in my opinion, the single best book ever written on the subject of negotiation." See "Divorce and Family Medicine," in Sandole and Sandole-Staroste, eds., *Conflict Management and Problem Solving*, 112.

28   Fisher and Ury, *Getting to Yes*, xii. Also see Raiffa, *The Art and Science of Negotiation*.

29   On the links between moral norms meaning schemes, see Melchin, "Moral Knowledge and the Structure of Cooperative Living."

30   Fisher and Ury, *Getting to Yes*, 14.

31   Ibid., 10.

32   Ibid., 10-14.

33   Ibid., 17-22.

34   Ibid., 22-40.

35   See George Herbert Mead, *On Social Psychology: Selected Papers*, ed. Anselm Strauss (Chicago: University of Chicago Press, 1964), 33-40, 209-22. Also see Gibson Winter, *Elements for a Social Ethic* (New York: Macmillan, 1966), 88-109; and Melchin, *History, Ethics, and Emergent Probability*, 181-87.

36   Fisher and Ury, *Getting to Yes*, 23.

37   See Melchin, *History, Ethics, and Emergent Probability*, 181-87.

38   See, for example, Frank Fincham, Steven Beach, and Donald Baucom, "Attribution Processes in Distressed and Nondistressed Couples: 4. Self-Partner Attribution Differences," *Journal of Personality and Social Psychology* 52 (1987): 739-48.

39   For an introduction to techniques and skills which can be used to clarify intended meaning, see Fisher and Brown, *Getting Together*. For an introduction to techniques and skills which third parties can implement to help disputants clarify intended meaning see Moore, *The Mediation Process*, 153-98.

40   Fisher and Ury, *Getting to Yes*, 41-57.

41   Also see Moore, *The Mediation Process*, 198.

42   On the role of feelings in family mediation, see Gaugan in Sandole and Sandole-Staroste, eds., *Conflict Management*, 110-17.

43   On the significance of recognizing diverse interests as legitimate see Elizabeth Koopman, "Family Mediation: A Developmental Perspective on the Field," in Sandole and Sandole-Staroste eds., *Conflict Management*, 120.

44   Lonergan, *Insight*, 217.

45   On the role of "integrative agreements" in negotiation, see Dean Pruitt, "Creative Approaches to Negotiation," in Sandole and Sandole-Staroste, eds., *Conflict Management*, 68-75.

46   Fisher and Ury, *Getting to Yes*, 58-83.

47   For some introductory discussions of this evidence, see Robert Axelrod, *The Evolution of Cooperation* (New York: Basic Books, 1984).

48   Fisher and Ury, *Getting to Yes*, 62-64.

49   Bernard Lonergan, *Method in Theology* (New York: Herder and Herder, 1972), chap.1.

50   For further discussion of the role of cooperative behaviour in promoting further cooperation, see Morton Deutsch, "A Theoretical Perspective on Conflict and Conflict Resolution," in Sandole and Sandole-Staroste eds., *Conflict Management*, 38-49; and Tetsuo Kondo, "Some Notes on Rational Behaviour, Normative Behaviour, Moral Behaviour, and Cooperation," *Journal of Conflict Resolution* 34 (1990): 495-530.

51   Fisher and Ury, *Getting to Yes*, 84-98.

52   Ibid., 101-49.

53   Ibid., 134.

54   See, for example, Kenneth R. Melchin, "The Challenges of Technological Society for an Understanding of Christian Faith," in Jacques Croteau ed., *Défis présents et à venir de l'université catholique/Present and Future Challenges Facing Catholic Universities* (Ottawa: Saint Paul University, 1990), 123-38.

Five

Welcoming the Other: The Philosophical Foundations for Pluralism in the Works of Charles Davis and Emmanuel Levinas

MICHAEL OPPENHEIM

There is perhaps no need more pressing in civilization today than the fostering of an acceptance and appreciation for persons who are different than oneself. The evidence of the failure of toleration and respect for the other is omnipresent and sometimes overwhelming. This is particularly, but not exclusively, the case in the context of the encounter between different religious cultures. It often seems that those institutions, systems of belief and action that express humanity's longing for relation with the Ultimate also embody or direct their most extreme hatred and violence toward those who are different.

In reaction to this state of affairs, to the violence that persons within one religious group sometimes express toward those from another group, there are religious persons who have written and worked to liberate us all from the destructive passions of intolerance and hatred. Charles Davis and Emmanuel Levinas are two such men. They are religious thinkers who have been shocked by the violence inflicted on the other and have attempted to demonstrate the necessity and the grounds for a passionate religious commitment to pluralism.

While Davis and Levinas have made the theme of the acceptance or appreciation of the other an important element in their work, there are profound differences in the ways that they pursue this task. The differences reflect both the traditions out of which they speak as well as their own individualities as modern religious thinkers. In exploring their understandings of the nature of and foundations for religious pluralism, I believe we will learn of some of the concerns, values, and hopes that animate their thought. We will also come to appreciate the "plurality" of approaches that can be taken toward the conception of pluralism itself.

I

Before examining Davis's understanding of and argument for pluralism, it is important to recognize that there are perhaps two different contexts for his treatment of this issue. First, pluralism has a place within his examination of the challenges that modernity forces upon the Catholic Church and Christianity more widely. Second, pluralism also is a theme in his analysis of the nature of religion and the problems that beset all religious traditions in our time.

It is in his major work *Christ and the World Religions* (1970) that Davis begins to address the issue of religious pluralism from a specific Christian perspective: "The general problem I want to tackle here is the relation between faith in Jesus Christ and the other religious options still drawing allegiance from men."[1] Davis recognizes that for both theologians and laypersons the issues are new. His standpoint is within the Christian tradition, as a Christian, but the truth and claims of Christianity are seen by him as legitimate matters at issue. This argument reveals a fundamental aspect of Davis's discussion of religious pluralism as a whole. It embodies his effort to critique Christian exclusivism, and to open the way toward an authentic but critical appreciation of the variety and vitality of all of the religious endeavours of humans.[2] This effort is continued in *Theology and Political Society* and *What Is Living, What Is Dead in Christianity Today?* where he reiterates this theme as the need to move away from the "parochial exclusiveness of most Christian theologians, whether Catholic or Protestant."[3]

While as a Christian theologian Davis has been primarily concerned with the necessity of overcoming various strains of Christian exclusiveness, he also has spoken about similar elements in other religious traditions. In such essays as "Our New Religious Identity," "The Philosophical Foundations of Pluralism," and "The Political Use and Misuse of Religious Language," pluralism within the context of the world's religions is explored. In these smaller writings, there are analyses of the nature of the religious experience as well as statements about the emerging basis that permits us to question the claims of exclusivity in all traditions.

What are the motivations that compel Davis to wrestle with this theme in so many works? There is his feeling of responsibility as a theologian that the future of Christian communities is imperiled today unless authentic responses to the challenges of modernity can be fashioned. More particularly, he believes that religious exclusivity limits the open quest of humans to converse with each other, preventing individuals and traditions from learning and sharing with each other. Without a respect for the other, humans are impeded in their ongoing, mutual effort to discover truth and create meaning. More pointedly and more dangerously, he seems to feel that religious exclusivity leads to a defensiveness and fanaticism that always has the potential of exploding into violence.

In his explorations of the nature of pluralism, Davis insists that there must be an area of unity among persons, some unity within or despite the diversity. In his words:

> Pluralism, then, also implies unity, some consensus or agreement. The divergent groups form one community; they agree to live together and co-operate in action for common goals. Pluralism is not brute plurality. It means harmony amid discord, unity of social life and political action amid religious and valuation conflict.[4]

The matter of religious pluralism is more complex. However, one dimension of the unity that allows for an authentic religious pluralism can be recognized in his contention, following the work of Wilfred Cantwell Smith, that there is "the convergence of the various traditions . . . towards the formation of a variegated, critical, global self-consciousness in which we come together in communication and partnership."[5]

Davis's understanding of pluralism also evidences a recognition that a significant way of experiencing the world is found among those who value this concept. He writes that "pluralism is the response of finite intelligence to a reality so rich that it constantly escapes its categories and calls for the convergence and complementarity of various cultures and modes of expressions."[6] Again, the idea that there is a developing unity, or at least, convergence and complementarity among humans, is brought out.

From another angle, the meaning of pluralism within Davis's corpus emerges by examining what seems to stand as its opposite. Pluralism is often discussed, if not defined, in terms of its opposites, that is, particularity and exclusiveness. He speaks of "parochial exclusiveness,"[7] of the need to overcome "the exclusive particularity of a supernaturally instituted Christian religion"[8] and, more generally, of the thrust in mystical religion that "compels one to find the universal in the particular and to move from exclusiveness to pluralism."[9]

The argument for pluralism, its justification as it were, takes two different directions in Davis's writing. The discussion of the convergence and complementarity of the major religious traditions is one basis for pluralism. The other is provided by an analysis of the nature of religious experience. The conclusion that no religious tradition is justifiable in affirming that it and only it possesses the truth because there is a developing common religious consciousness or identity that supersedes such affirmations, is the climax of the first argument. In the second, the contention that the experience of the transcendent is basically negative grounds his understanding that no religious group can claim that its symbols, doctrines, etc., are absolute.

There are a number of texts that discuss the emerging new religious identity or convergence of religious traditions. In *Theology and Political Society*, Davis utilizes, with critical reservations, some of the work of Jürgen Habermas. Habermas speaks of the social evolution of ego and group identity in terms of stages. He describes different points within the history of cultures and religious traditions and isolates trends in the development from one stage to the next. The trends in the development of humanity's social identity include: the expansion of the secular in relation to the sacred; the movement toward autonomy; the shift from particularism to universalistic and individualized orientation; and the increasing reflexivity of belief.[10] In the final stage, one sees an identity not tied to a particular place or territory, but in terms of mutual participation in an ongoing communication process where a collective will and identity take shape.

Davis's understanding of the newly emerging religious identity is guided by the treatment of social identity that Habermas presents. He bases this view on an understanding of religious history not as the histories of discrete and completed entities, but as a "single history of human religiousness."[11] He also sees a convergence of religious traditions, implying "the end of orthodoxy, in the sense of a religious identity mediated through the fixed, objectified contents of a particular religious tradition."[12] More positively, this convergence marks a uniting of people of different traditions and positions in a growing inclusive religious communication. There is a "sharing of life. People are learning to live together, to listen to one another's stories, to interpret and become familiar with alien symbols, to respect different customs and join in the rites of others."[13] This sharing of living and learning does not, in Davis's view, mean the end of specific religious traditions or the appearance of some abstract, universal discourse. Rather, it "articulates a unity of communication in the lasting differences of historical experience and remembrance and consequently of traditions, though these remain under a constant process of development and revision."[14]

In the article of 1980, "Our New Religious Identity," the link between the newly developing identity and the convergence of religious traditions is reaffirmed. He writes:

> Making one's own the ongoing, convergent history of religious faith by participating in a process of free, equal, and universal communication among people striving without domination to reach agreement on religious concerns is how one achieves a basic social identity of a religious kind at the level of the resent situation.[15]

Here, too, an appreciation for pluralism of religions and not some abstract universalism is acknowledged. He finds that there is a need for particular traditions to ground individuals, to provide for personal growth and to express the rich individuality of religious faith.

If one approach that Davis takes to the issue of pluralism is in terms of identity and history, the second complements this by addressing pluralism within the context of what might be called a philosophical analysis of the nature of religious experience. The treatment of the human encounter with the transcendent as the basis for pluralism is developed in the text *Christ and the World Religions*.

Davis holds that religious faith is the outcome of a person being grasped by the ultimate or transcendent. It is a "gift," which probably means both a mystery and something not within human control. It is important to note that for the author, the development of faith takes place in "subjective consciousness." It is not "necessarily" the product of some historical encounter. He speaks of a person's "attempts to objectify the data of his subjective consciousness as modified by the presence of the transcendent," and continues that the "various symbolic forms of faith are objectifications produced by the human psyche in its reaction to its non-objective union with the transcendent."[16] Thus, the symbolic and doctrinal expressions of religion are seen as human products resulting from the inner "union" with the transcendent. Corresponding to this notion of the symbolic forms of religion, is the affirmation that religion cannot offer us anything that might be called a "proper knowledge of the transcendent itself."[17] Human thought and speech are brought to silence by this reality, and even symbols can only "reach out into the unknown."[18] Such symbols can, in fact, be critiqued. They can be judged in terms of the extent to which they "measure up to the height and depth and breadth of human experience."[19]

In *Christ and the World Religions*, Davis's position is firmly that of a Christian theologian who is committed to the Christian tradition, and to the "universality and finality of Christ."[20] This affirmation does not disallow for other religions, for "faith in Christ . . . does not . . . imply a denial of the persisting function of other religions in God's ordering of history or of the positive value of religious pluralism."[21] The case for pluralism, in this instance the importance of dialogue with other traditions in the present, is also made by Davis through a reference to the past. He cites the impact of non-Christian mystic movements on the development and flowering of medieval Christian mysticism as an example of the way that such dialogue can lead to new understandings and insights. The last section of this book restates Davis's contention that no single view of Christ or of the historical working of God is final. This follows from his understanding of the nature of religious faith and the products of such faith. However, within the perspective of this work, he does not insist upon the symbolic, and thus, limited nature of the foundational Christian belief in Christ. The "universality and finality of Christ" for Christians remains a basic tenet of his position.

There is a parallel discussion of religious experience and pluralism in a later essay, "The Political Use and Misuse of Religious Language" (1989), which, it seems to me, brings forward a somewhat different conclusion than the earlier treatment. The point of departure for this article is the use or *misuse* of religion or religious faith to buttress particular political positions. Davis argues that religious experience does not issue in some kind of specific content of meaning or knowledge that can then be directly applied to our life in the world. God is essentially a mystery, and "the fundamental experience of the transcendent is negative in the sense of an absence of formulable meaning." This understanding entails that the "positive elements of meaning are deabsolutized and rendered dispensable."[22]

The proposition that "the experience of the transcendent in faith is fundamentally negative in the sense that it brings us no proper content of meaning"[23] is very important in Davis's argument for religious pluralism. There can be no direct conflict between faith statements or claims among religions because all faith statements are both human and tentative. None is absolute. Further, even symbol systems cannot be said to collide or exclude each other in some absolute sense. While it is true that no specific content issues from the experience of the transcendent, symbol and myth are legitimate reactions to or expressions of that experience. Nevertheless, even these are not final or themselves transcendent. This leads Davis to discuss what he terms the "principle of equivalence of symbols," which means that "the truth and efficacy of one symbolic system does not exclude the truth and efficacy of other, different systems."[24] Additional insights that underlie religious pluralism are presented in the essay, but this one, it seems to me, is the keystone.

My perception is that the divergence between the two discussions of pluralism in *Christ and the World Religions* and in the article "The Political Use and Misuse of Religious Language" rests on the treatment of Christ as that which embodies the Christian experience of the transcendent. In the book, Davis speaks of Christ's universality and finality for Christian faith, while in the essay it seems that no religious symbol or system should be understood in this way. The difference in the two writings may be explored in a variety of ways. The first is directed to the Christian community, while the second is addressed to scholars of Christianity, and possibly other traditions. In the first, the author endeavours to bring committed Christians to see the value and importance of other religious communities. In the second, the issue of pluralism is not tackled from within the Christian community. There is also the possibility of development in Davis's understanding or critique of religious symbols. In any case, I will take the later essay, which conforms to other recent writings more than the earlier book, as the more fully developed position concerning religious pluralism.

The discussions of pluralism in terms of the developing common religious identity or convergence of religions, and in terms of the characterization of the experience of the transcendent, complement each other. First, one discussion explores modern social and cultural developments and their effects on religion, while the other examines the nature of religious experience itself. Second, both dimensions of religious life are brought together in the author's recent considerations of the mystical principle in religion. He holds that the developing common religious identity has been made possible because of the modern views about religious experience that are in some sense influenced by mystic understandings.

The mystical dimension of religion is a theme that appears in a number of Davis's works of the last decade, including *What Is Living, What Is Dead in Christianity Today?* A central place in the book is given over to a discussion of four major models of Christianity: the mystic, mythical, pragmatic, and visionary. The author is very critical of the mythical model of Christianity in this work. His presentation of it corresponds to the ways that he describes orthodox or traditional views of religion in other contexts. The mythical model of Christianity is seen as very literal. It takes phenomenon and events in human history and directly relates them to the cosmic order. Religious institutions are held to be unchangeable and independent of human development. The mythic model of Christianity rejects other religious communities as competitors because it identifies particular institutions and beliefs with an eternal, supernatural order. He sees the threat posed to pluralism by mythic conceptions of Christianity and other traditions in the following terms: "Myth of its nature is exclusive and coercive, because it is a social charter that articulates an objective order, independent of human volition. There is no room for pluralism that allows equal validity to other accounts of reality."[25]

The mystic model stands in opposition to the mythic one. This model includes the view that the "union with God" is the ultimate goal of religion and it treats all the instruments that lead to and from this goal as secondary. These instruments or mediating elements are not important in themselves and can be left behind or replaced. In terms of Christianity proper, this version relativizes and treats as replaceable all that is distinctly Christian.[26]

The mystic understanding of religious experience has played a role in the development of the understanding of many modern religious persons. It has brought people to see that while the world's religions embody a plethora of different symbol systems, there may be a common experience of the ineffable beneath this diversity. This point is forcefully made by the author in terms of Christianity:

It was the mystical principle that enabled modern thinkers to overcome the exclusive particularity of a supernaturally instituted Christian religion and to interpret Christian religious experience in the context of the unity in pluralism of the religious history of humankind.[27]

II

The issue of pluralism is very prominent in the works of Emmanuel Levinas. It plays an important role is his two major books, *Totality and Infinity* and *Otherwise than Being or Beyond Essence,* and arises throughout his individual essays. It is so important to the overall oeuvre that if one wanted an entrée into Levinas's thought, the concern for and treatment of pluralism would be fully sufficient.

The word pluralism (*le pluralisme*) has very special and specific uses in Levinas's work. One sense of this meaning can be heard in a statement from the autobiographical essay "Signature." He writes: "Time, language and subjectivity delineate a pluralism and consequently, in the strongest sense of this term, an experience: one being's reception of an absolutely other being."[28] Pluralism is the name that is given to the experience of one person confronting or facing another where the other demands, as it were, to remain separate or other. More accurately, Levinas speaks of the self receiving the other, which underscores his view that the encounter does not arise out of the subject's will to power or even good will, but from its being confronted. It is the other person who acts upon, who impinges upon my controlled world, who demands. The self of I is passive. In *Totality and Infinity*, this notion of pluralism is restated and, at the same time contrasted, with the notion of a mere "numerical multiplicity." Unlike this arithmetic reference, pluralism "implies a radical alterity of the other, whom I do not simply *conceive* by relation to myself, but *confront* out of my egoism."[29]

Another dimension can be seen, from the same text, in a peculiar use of the cognate term "plurality"; "sexuality in us is neither knowledge nor power, but the very plurality of our existing."[30] He means by this that sexuality cannot be adequately analyzed as the self's search for pleasure: it is a relation to someone beyond, someone "absolutely other," someone who can never be "converted into 'mine.' "[31] Sexuality, and his term "fecundity," denote one aspect of human pluralism: the fact that we are oriented toward a separate other who can never be turned into just another aspect of myself.

While the more individual, phenomenological use of the term pluralism occurs frequently in different texts, a wider social sense of the term can be gleaned here and there. At the end of *Totality and Infinity* there is a statement about the nature of pluralist society. Such a society evidences "the unity of plurality." Pluralist society stands upon relations of true pluralism, that is, upon the respect and responsibility that the self expresses toward the other. There is a unity here, but that unity is once again contrasted with any mere numerical or systematic grouping-totality. Ultimately, authentic peace is "the unity of plurality" for Levinas.[32]

It can be said that pluralism motivates Levinas's entire philosophical endeavour, just as a whole ethics, philosophical anthropology, philosophy of language and epistemology arise out of the dynamics of facing the other. A concise and powerful expression—which is his way—of the passion behind the enterprise appears in the dedication to *Otherwise than Being or Beyond Essence*: "To the memory of those who were closest among the six million assassinated by the National Socialists, and of the millions on millions of all confessions and all nations, victims of the same hatred of the other man, the same anti-semitism."[33] Beyond the usual interests of ethics, epistemology, and even aesthetics, thus stands a fundamentally ethical-political concern. We will soon turn to the explication of this relationship between philosophy and politics, or what he terms philosophy and the state.

Levinas's commitment to or responsibility for present-day Jewish communities is also a motive for his insistence on the significance of pluralism. His commitment has led to essays both indicating the continued relevance of the Jewish past for modern Jews and non-Jews, and expressing the need for the Jewish community to successfully interact with non-Jewish cultures. Succinctly he writes: "Loyalty to a Jewish culture closed to dialogue and polemic with the West condemns the Jews to the ghetto and to physical extermination."[34]

The present treatment of pluralism in Levinas will explore both the philosophical texts and the writings dedicated to Jewish life in our times. One scholar of the philosophical work has commented that "Levinas's proposals offer about as extreme a form of radical pluralism as has appeared in Western philosophy."[35] Since pluralism in this respect refers to the encounter between self and other, Levinas's position is radical because it affirms as insistently and consistently as possible that the other must remain separate from the self. The language of this insistence is shocking to the traditional philosopher. The encounter with the other is the confrontation with "transcendence" or "Infinity," and the need for the other is nothing less than "metaphysical desire."

Levinas is a provocateur: his work acts as a challenge to a natural human tendency or movement of the self to include or contain the other.

According to him, the individual seeks to incorporate all that is different from the self, all alterity, into a single, total system of thought and life that is coterminous with himself or herself. The self works to replace alterity with "the same." The endeavour to eliminate or eradicate the other has both a philosophical and a political expression, according to Levinas. For him, the history of philosophy is just this history of incorporating alterity within a total framework of being or ontology. Philosophers of ontology seek to present a system, in terms of the language of being, in which everything is included. Through this effort all that is individual, particular, and other is overcome. Said in another way, the philosophy of ontology is the philosophy of domination.

The connection between philosophy and the state is reaffirmed throughout Levinas's work. Philosophy presents a logic, a justification, that both leads to and underwrites the political effort to unite all persons in some common entity. While to those who philosophize or hold power this effort looks benign or even "enlightened," from the perspective of those who are not the dominant group, the violence toward the other is all too real. The argument is sometimes put very tersely by Levinas. He writes that "Ontology as first philosophy is a philosophy of power. It issues in the State and in the nonviolence of the totality . . . which appears in the tyranny of the State."[36]

This argument can be put in another way. The distrust of a single rational order, whether system or movement, rests upon Levinas's view of the interrelationship between philosophy and the state. Western philosophy has continually recognized as its "destiny," according to Levinas, the forging of an all-encompassing discourse out of the multiplicity of authentic discourses. This self-understanding corresponds, on the political side, to what he terms "the march towards universality of a political order." However, whether theoretical or political, both movements rest upon the violent supersession of the individual and the particular.[37]

If ontology is a "philosophy of power," then the rejection of this can only come by way of a new point of departure for philosophy. "Ethics as First Philosophy" is the title of one of Levinas's most important essays. The ethical critique of philosophy and politics is founded on the absolute recognition of the integrity of the other person. Levinas speaks of this in terms of the idea of Infinity. The idea of infinity is, first of all, not something that one can give oneself, according to Levinas. Utilizing the analysis of Descartes, he holds that the idea of infinity surpasses everything

I can engender. Second, it testifies to the height of the other that escapes all of the self's efforts to measure or put into some usable perspective.

Levinas holds that the encounter with the other is prior not only to ontology and epistemology, it is prior to self-consciousness. My recognition of myself as a particular being is built upon my situation, and thus the human situation, of hearing the outside voice of the other and being responsible to her or him. In the words of Levinas, it is "my inescapable and incontrovertible answerability to the other that makes me an individual 'I.' "[38] The nature of the self 's response to the other is portrayed by Levinas in terms of the face to face encounter. The face of the other is a revelation. It reveals the poverty and vulnerability of all humans. In the face one sees the plight of the poor and the stranger. However, Levinas is not interested in what feelings the face of the other might evoke. The face of the one whom I confront cries out with demands. Primary here is the command not to kill.

It is important to note that the phenomenology of face to face gives primacy not just to responsibility and response, but to speech. For Levinas, language and speech are not the outcome of self-consciousness or the expression of prior reflection or thinking. They constitute the first, the natural matrix for my life. "Face and discourse are tied. The face speaks. It speaks, it is in this that it renders possible and begins all discourse . . . it is discourse and, more exactly, response or responsibility which is this authentic relationship."[39]

Levinas grounds reason in speech rather than speech in reason. Speech represents for him the whole phenomenology of self confronting the other. Further, speech, unlike reason, does not attempt to overcome separation. Levinas is not naive: he recognizes that speech is not immune from the tendencies to systematize and to reduce alterity to the same. Yet, he believes that ever again the primal situation of standing face to face as well as the authentic speech of responsibility bursts out of the chrysalis of the same. On the one hand, Levinas warns that every communication that is not based upon responsibility is an effort in domination.[40] On the other hand, he indicates that there is a fundamental connection between language and alterity. He writes that "the relationship of language implies transcendence, radical separation, the strangeness of the interlocutors, the revelation of the other to me."[41]

Levinas's writings on the relationship between Judaism and other traditions as well as his reflections on pluralism within society are primarily found within the collection *Difficile Liberté*. The critique of philosophical and theological positions that find comfort in some variety of universalism resounds within essays written over decades. The following passage recognizes that violence has resulted from the confrontations between particular exclusivist communities. However, its primary focus is another strain of violence; that oppressive violence of purported universalisms:

> Between the wars which emerged from particularisms and the violence of those which seek to reduce them to a State, is there not a place for an absolutely pacifist and apolitical universalism? It would perhaps consist in loving men rather than being concerned about their discourse; in not constructing one's truth from the shavings of the opinions one has come up against; in not recognizing the progress of Reason in successive examples of human madness, or eternal structures in the fragile institutions of ephemeral states.[42]

One prerequisite of this apolitical, subversive universalism is brought out above. It consists of focusing on the relations among persons and groups and not on beliefs and opinions. Suspicious of universal reason, Levinas defines a truly nonviolent universalism in terms of mutual respect.

Does this mean that Levinas refuses to acknowledge the goal of having groups overcome the individuality of their discourse in order to both participate in something wider and surpass their own particularity? The answer is yes. In fact, he holds that the destiny of Israel to remain a people apart, stands for the truth, the ethical necessity of rejecting the wider and the surpassing.

Difficile Liberté defines this stance of Israel, this testimony to authentic universalism. We have already seen that one element of this "pacifist universalism" is respect for the other as well as a concern with moral actions rather than agreement about beliefs. Levinas's description of Israel among the nations confirms these points. Like Christianity and Islam, it is an expression of monotheism. Monotheism, in Levinas's view, is not a matter of arithmetic. Monotheism implies, first, that there is one God who unites all humans as brothers and sisters. As Levinas formulates it, monotheism is the "supernatural gift of seeing that one man is absolutely like another man beneath the variety of historical traditions kept alive in each case."[43] More powerfully, it points to the realm of obligations. God is the one who issues the call to help the neighbour and stranger, the call of obligation. Monotheism affirms that the other cannot be ignored, that the self cannot refuse to enter into discourse.[44] The discourse is the discourse of responsibility. Here persons can share concerns, and move one another.

Yet Levinas is not eager to share faith and exchange beliefs among traditions or communities. The universalism that he affirms is, in his terms, the universalism of "serving the universe" which remains in the realm of ethics.[45]

Levinas speaks of Israel as a blend of universal and particular that stands for all humankind. It is universal, in ways it shares with other monotheistic traditions, in speaking of the fraternity of all humans and responsibility for the other. It is universal in the sense that it is open to all. Further, it rejects any hierarchy of traditions. In the language of the rabbis, this is stated as the just of all nations shall have a place in the world to come. He comments:

> The rabbinic principle by which the just of every nation participate in
> the future world expresses not only an eschatological view. It affirms
> the possibility of that ultimate intimacy, beyond the dogma affirmed by
> the one or the other, an intimacy without reserve.[46]

Israel's particularity is found within the shocking concept of "election." Levinas does not hesitate to refer to it, but insists it means not privileges but responsibilities. The Jewish people has been given special obligations, "exceptional duties."[47] The universality of Judaism does not contradict its particularity, as Levinas sees it. He does not shun, despite all that we have heard above, the use of the term "exclusivity." He writes: "The fact that tolerance can be inherent in religion without religion losing its exclusivity is perhaps the meaning of Judaism, which is a religion of tolerance."[48]

III

In the foregoing I have tried to portray the positions of Charles Davis and Emmanuel Levinas in their own terms. I have attempted to elucidate the understanding of the nature of pluralism, the motivations for discussion, and the different philosophical justifications or arguments. Although, on first reflection, one might have assumed that the positions of two contemporary religious thinkers on the issue of pluralism would exhibit many areas of agreement, it is the differences that are the most striking.[49] These concern not only the basic definition of the issue itself, the reasons why pluralism is required, and the relationship between particularity and universality, but also those subjects that each regards as relevant to a discussion of pluralism. Beyond even these, there are also less obvious but interesting and telling differences in terms of treatments of the nature of religious experience and symbols, speech and the body.

The vocabulary of pluralism that occurs within the two discourses represent one of the most significant differences. This is evident in the use and relationships between such terms as universalism, particularity, and exclusivity. In the discussions that take place within Davis's texts, pluralism is tied to the universal. The twin terms particularity and exclusivity are often found together and are presented as opposed to pluralism. The statement about the need to "find the universal in the particular and to move from exclusiveness to pluralism," is the best example of this overall expression. Further, the particular is often portrayed in contrast to the universal as both parochial and limited, as in the expression "tribal particularism."[50]

Davis believes that the major threat to pluralism arises out of the clash of exclusivist claims made by groups of traditions that maintain that only they possess the truth or are in a relationship with the divine. He critiques those who propose the "exclusive particularity of a supernaturally instituted Christian religion."[51] He holds that this threat can become obsolete as people recognize that there is an expanding religious consciousness that straddles the boundaries of particular traditions and brings forward communication and religious insights that unite humans. Thus, the hope of pluralism rests upon unity, upon what can be shared among persons. Davis acknowledges that humans are born and nurtured in particular traditions and need the symbols and rituals of those traditions to maintain a concrete identity. However, it is not a distortion to suggest that he envisions a pluralism *despite particularity*. In his words, "pluralism is not brute plurality."[52]

Levinas's presentation and argument are much different. His discussions of the meaning of pluralism always introduce such expressions as the "absolutely other being,"[53] and the "radical alterity of the other."[54] Authentic pluralism does not overcome the particular. In fact, he can even use the term "exclusivity" in a positive way as was the case in his description of Judaism as being "a religion of tolerance" that did not lose its "exclusivity."[55] The universal is often placed in opposition to pluralism as in his statement about "the march towards universality of a political order."[56] Universalism is customarily defined in terms of totality and violence. It becomes something positive when combined with the "particular" where the latter dominates. I have in mind the example of Levinas's oxymoronic description of a "universalist particularism" that he finds in Zionism.[57]

Although Levinas perceives the violence that has resulted from the clash of individual groups, his discussion is most sensitive to the violence that is the outcome of the suppression of particular groups of cultures. He believes that domination often occurs or is justified through the discourse of universalism; of what all persons share. For him, on the contrary, pluralism rests on the mutual respect of separate individuals and groups that encounter one another, each recognizing the integrity of the other. While traditions may share specific ethical concerns or orientations, especially as the outcome of monotheism, his hope for the peace of pluralism rests on behaviour, respect and toleration, rather than on common views. Overall, he offers a vision of pluralism *requiring particularity.*

There are contrasting views of the nature of religious experience which seem to ground, philosophically, the divergent treatments of particularity and universalism. It is noteworthy that this ground is more developed in Davis's work than in Levinas's. Put in another way, it appears that Davis finds that his treatment of pluralism requires a thorough analysis of religious experience, revelation, and their relationship to tradition, while Levinas does not feel a need for the same analysis in the context of his presentation.

The term mystic or mysticism plays a prominent role in Davis's discussion of pluralism. For example, there is the statement that it was the "mystical principle that enabled modern thinkers to overcome the exclusive particularity of a supernaturally instituted Christian religion."[58] For Davis, contact with the transcendent is not a matter of some outside event in the world. Such contact takes place in "subjective consciousness without necessarily any objective revelation."[59] God is essentially a mystery and there is no concrete knowledge of the absolute. In his words, the "fundamental experience of the transcendent is negative in the sense of an absence of formulable meaning."[60] The implication of this understanding is fully stated by him: "the positive elements of meaning (in a religious tradition) are deabsolutized and rendered dispensable."[61] Davis sees that when this view of religious experience is shared by persons in different traditions, they are enabled to step beyond the specific symbols, faith statements, and institutions.

There is no fully corresponding statement about religious experience and tradition in the discourse on pluralism by Levinas. Still, Levinas's understanding of Torah differs greatly from the way that Davis discusses the relationship between religious experience and symbols. For Levinas, Torah is the result of an event of revelation. In this event, there was both divine and human input. While Torah is in human words, it is more than a human product. This means that one cannot get behind or beyond Torah. It is not relative. It is not dispensable. As he writes in a rather recent essay, "Revelation in the Jewish Tradition" (1977): "The Talmud affirms the prophetic and verbal origin of the Revelation, but lays more emphasis on the voice of the person listening. It is as if the Revelation were a system of signs to be interpreted by the auditor and, in this sense, already handed over to him."[62] Levinas is neither a fundamentalist, nor a literalist. He does not affirm, for example, that the Torah is all the work of one author, Moses. The miracle of its authorship, as he puts it, is not a matter of such purported authorship but of the amazing consistency and power of its message: the "confluence of different literatures toward the same essential content."[63]

However, one cannot philosophically go behind the text and see it as mere human creation. Levinas reverts to what might be called story to say what can be said here. One key to understanding this is embodied in the phrase "as if," in the statement quoted above about revelation. The phrase plays a role similar to the Rabbinic phrase "*ka'ba yahol*," "as it were." Revelation is neither an objective system of signs nor is it not such a system. One can say, in a particular context, it is "as if " it were.

Thus, one reason that Davis speaks of a converging religious identity is that he understands that it is possible to identify a common core of religious experience that lies behind and relativizes all specific religious expressions, that is, religious symbols, texts, and institutions. Levinas rejects both the converging identity and the view that it is possible to speak of a common religious experience that transcends and enables one to step beyond symbols within traditions.

Another important illustration of the opposing views concerns the religious symbol that is central to many traditions, God. More specifically, there is a disagreement about the significance of understanding God as a discrete other, perhaps, as "person." An analysis of "theism" appears in a number of Davis's works, especially *Body as Spirit* and *Theology and Political Society*. In the latter, he summarizes his position:

> I do not consider negligible the difference between a mystical oneness that preserves the distinction of a person God and the individual human being and a mystical oneness that identifies the self and Ultimate Reality without distinction. I also think that theism has made possible the emergence of the individual self in a way that other forms of religion have not.[64]

Nevertheless, in the more extended treatment he has written that, "God if it is not made an idol, must be recognized as merely an inadequate, analogical expression, mediating a thrust toward a directly inexpressible mystery that lies beyond any human conception."[65] This view of theism is fully consistent with his treatment of religious symbols and concepts. The religious symbol that the theist calls God is an important element in some traditions. The symbol has both meaning and religious implications. However, the symbol is an "inadequate" expression of an experience of "inexpressible mystery." In other words, it is still important to see it as relative and a secondary expression of a core religious experience.

Levinas does not have a parallel treatment of the theistic notion of God. In fact, there is great reticence to explore the notion of God or the experience of God directly in his literature. This is one of the most distinguishing features of both his philosophical and religious literature. I find that the indirectness of his God-language is not the result of his understanding of this symbol as relative or secondary, but that it, among other things, prevents or disallows the type of philosophical analysis that appears in the writings of Davis. The indirectness of this God-language is fully apparent in the following:

> Ethics is an optics of the Divine. Henceforth, no relation with God is direct or immediate. The Divine can be manifested only through my neighbour.[66]

> The Other is not the incarnation of God, but precisely by his face, in which he is disincarnate, is the manifestation of the height in which God is revealed.[67]

God stands as an entity distinct from, but assessable through humans. Just as ethics requires the separation and integrity of self and other, so the religious life continues this principle. Levinas's discourse prevents the possibility of privileging some direct experience of the divine reality and thus stepping beyond tradition, symbol, and word.

There is a large divergence in the treatment of language or speech which follows upon the fault lines that have been surveyed in other areas. While both thinkers value discourse and communication very highly, they differ in their understandings of what is most important about such discourse and what are the overall powers of speech. Davis is particularly interested in the way that communication brings people together, bridges differences, and allows people to share experiences and insights. He speaks of the "free, equal, and universal communication among people,"[68] and of the "structure of communication now growing among the religious communities."[69]

Levinas sees the need for a shared discourse, at least in terms of ethics. However, as persistent as this point is, there is also a suspicion of a more far-reaching sharing. He discusses the "march towards universality of a political order" in terms of "confronting multiple beliefs—a multiplicity of coherent discourses—and finding one coherent discourse that embraces them all, which is precisely the universal order."[70] Additionally, Levinas is most interested in the fact that discourse respects the alterity of the other. He writes that "the relationship of language implies transcendence, radical separation, the strangeness of the interlocutors, the revelation of the other to me."[71]

In terms of the powers and limits of language, the two thinkers also stand apart. As we have seen, Davis believes that the experience of the transcendent brings speech to an end and, as an implication of this, any faith content is only a secondary reflection upon the inexpressible mystery of the transcendent. For Levinas, the transcendent appears exactly in the face to face of persons, which is synonymous with the act of speaking between persons. I find that Levinas's insistence on the divine dimension of Torah is in harmony with this view of the transcendent powers within speech.

Finally, there is some correspondence between the differences listed above and the role that the body or language of the body has in the discussions of pluralism.[72] I do not detect direct or metaphorical references to the body within Davis's discourse about pluralism. By now it is apparent that such references are essential to Levinas's presentation. What accounts for this absence in one case and presence in another? The body is the most expressive aspect in both a concrete and symbolic sense of the particularity of humans, and it therefore is not surprising that metaphors of the body are absent from a treatment that looks to a shared identity and convergence, and is present in one that demands the acknowledgement of the alterity of the other. Levinas's reference to sexuality in the context of a statement about pluralism is the strongest illustration of the tie that he sees: "sexuality in us is neither knowledge nor power, but the very plurality of our existing."[73]

The two approaches to pluralism surveyed above are very instructive. Among other conclusions that can be drawn is that the issue of pluralism requires many approaches and each of these may have their powers and limits. For example, Davis's stance provides us with a way of understanding and a language to describe the ways that traditions interact and learn from each other. It also proposes a perspective to overcome those exclusive aspects of traditions that often collide and lead to terrible conflict. Its weaknesses are well uncovered by Levinas's analysis. Every universalism is limited, and there is always the risk of violence towards those individuals and groups who do not recognize themselves within it.

Levinas's standpoint provides a philosophical basis for appreciating the integrity of each individual and group. It teaches us that the words peace and pluralism arise only where acts of respect and toleration abide. There is strength in its suspicion and its analysis of the correspondence between purported universal views, movements, and political powers. On the other hand, there are weaknesses in areas that mirror the strengths in the other treatment. For example, there is little in Levinas's discussion of the ways that different religious cultures have interacted in the past and have been deepened through such interaction. The fruitful possibilities of interreligious dialogue are not and cannot be explored very far by using the vocabulary of Levinas.

Some of the reasons for these two divergent treatments of pluralism have been touched upon throughout this discussion. We have seen differences in the problems that each thinker found to be foremost, in their audiences, and even in the definitions of pluralism offered. Certainly, each of these men is an independent thinker who powerfully colours whatever he studies and discusses. Still, that one stands as a Christian and another as a Jew cannot be dismissed as irrelevant.

It is not surprising for persons who have some acquaintance with the history and major expressions of the two traditions that the hope in the universal is highly prized in the work of a Christian philosopher and that a suspicion of the language of the universal, as well as an emphasis on the particular, occurs in the thought of a Jewish philosopher. Yet, there is more to see than such general tendencies. Many of the diagnostic positions that Davis holds are also to be found in the work of such contemporary Christian, and especially Catholic, theologians as Bernard Lonergan, Dominic Crossan, and David Tracy. This is especially true in the case of Crossan and Tracy in terms of the pivotal understanding of the subversive-disruptive, fundamentally negative experience of the divine. Remember that this understanding is essential to the argument that relativizes, but does not treat as irrelevant, all particular religious expressions.

The emphasis on the integrity of the particular, on the impossibility of stepping beyond the specific contents of a tradition is common to such modern Jewish philosophers as Franz Rosenzweig, Martin Buber, and others. Although they do not espouse a naive realism, fundamentalism, or literalism, they remain excited about the powers and not the limits of religious language. For them, the divine-human encounter, the encounter that issues in the covenant between two distinct "persons," remains the highest expression of religious life.

There are a variety of ways to think of and argue for religious pluralism. Charles Davis and Emmanuel Levinas present two of these. Their work reveals the complex issues and questions that must be addressed when one is combining a deep concern for pluralism with a life-commitment to one's own particular tradition. Additionally, the fact that we can recognize powers and limits within each of their portraits might well provide the basis for an argument about the necessity of a plurality of visions of pluralism.

Notes

1   Charles Davis, *Christ and the World Religions* (London: Hodder & Stoughton, 1970), 13.

2   Ibid., 130.

3   Charles Davis, *What Is Living, What Is Dead in Christianity Today? Breaking the Liberal-Conservative Deadlock* (San Francisco: Harper & Row, 1986), 2.

4   Charles Davis, "The Philosophical Foundations of Pluralism," in I. Beaubien, Charles Davis, Gilles Langevin, and Roger Lapointe, eds., *Le pluralism: Symposium inter-disciplinaire/Pluralism: Its Meaning Today* (Montréal: Fides, 1974), 223-24.

5   Davis, *What Is Living*, 1-2.

6   Ibid., 6.

7   Ibid., 2.

8   Ibid., 97.

9   Ibid.

10   Charles Davis, *Theology and Political Society* (Cambridge: Cambridge University Press, 1980), 163.

11   Ibid., 171.

12   Ibid., 172.

13   Ibid., 173.

14   Ibid., 174.

15   Charles Davis, "Our New Religious Identity," *Studies in Religion/Science Religieuses* 9 (Winter 1980): 37.

16   Davis, *Christ*, 113-14.

17   Ibid., 116.

18   Ibid., 114.

19   Ibid., 117.

20   Ibid., 127.

21   Ibid., 130.

22   Charles Davis, "The Political Use and Misuse of Religious Language," *Journal of Ecumenical Studies* 26 (Summer 1989): 486.

23   Ibid., 494.

24   Ibid.

25   Davis, *What Is Living*, 30.

26   Ibid., 51.

27   Ibid., 96-97.

28   Emmanuel Levinas, *Difficult Freedom: Essays on Judaism* (Baltimore: Johns Hopkins University Press, 1990), 293.

29   Emmanuel Levinas, *Totality and Infinity* (Pittsburgh: Duquesne University Press, 1969), 121. Italics in text.

30   Ibid., 227.

31   Ibid., 276.

32   Ibid., 306.

33   Emmanuel Levinas, *Otherwise than Being or Beyond Essence* (The Hague: Martinus Nijhoff, 1981), v.

34   Emmanuel Levinas, *Nine Talmudic Readings* (Bloomington: Indiana University Press, 1990), 9.

35   Harold A. Durfee, "War, Politics, and Radical Pluralism," *Philosophy and Phenomenological Research* 35 (1975): 556.

36   Levinas, *Totality*, 46.

37   Levinas, *Difficult Freedom*, 94.

38   Emmanuel Levinas and Richard Kearney, "Dialogue with Emmanual Levinas," in Richard A. Cohen, ed., *Face to Face with Levinas* (Albany: State University of New York Press, 1986), 27.

39   Emmanuel Levinas, *Ethics and Infinity: Conversations with Philippe Nemo* (Pittsburgh: Duquesne University Press, 1985), 87-88.

40   Levinas, *Otherwise*, 120.

41   Levinas, *Totality*, 73.

42   Levinas, *Difficult Freedom*, 239.

43   Ibid., 178.

44   Ibid., 178-79.

45   Ibid., 95.

46   Ibid., 176.

47   Ibid.

48   Ibid., 173.

49   While this essay has focused on the differences between these two thinkers, there is an important understanding about the foundations for pluralism that they share. In "The Philosophical Foundations of Pluralism" (249) Davis answered his own question in the negative, namely, whether "a genuine pluralism is a possibility without some form of belief in an ultimate reality beyond man." The belief in a transcendent reality is an extremely significant element in Davis's understanding of pluralism. Although Levinas does not directly discuss this issue, in light of his treatments of such topics as "the Other," "face to face," and the commandment not to kill, I find that his presentation of pluralism also rests on a belief in a transcendent reality. However, the differences in their views of the meaning of pluralism, the relationship to the transcendent and the nature of the transcendent retain their vitality here.

50   Davis, *Theology and Political Society*, 163.

51   Davis, *What Is Living*, 97.

52   Davis, "Philosophical Foundations," 223.

53   Levinas, *Difficult Freedom*, 293.

54   Levinas, *Totality*, 121.

55   Levinas, *Difficult Freedom*, 173.

56   Ibid., 94.

57   Ibid., 96.

58   Davis, *What Is Living*, 96-97.

59   Davis, *Christ*, 113.

60   Davis, "Political Use," 486.

61   Ibid.

62   Emmanuel Levinas, *The Levinas Reader*, ed. Sean Hand (Cambridge, MA: Basil Blackwell, 1989), 204.

63   Levinas, *Ethics and Infinity*, 115.

64   Davis, *Theology and Political Society*, 180.

65   Charles Davis, *Body as Spirit: The Nature of Religious Feeling* (New York: Seabury Press, 1976), 28.

66   Levinas, *Difficult Freedom*, 159.

67   Levinas, *Totality*, 79.

68   Davis, "Religious Identity," 37.

69   Davis, *Theology and Political Society*, 173.

70   Levinas, *Difficult Freedom*, 94.

71   Levinas, *Totality*, 73.

72   The correspondence between treatments of speech and the body in modern religious thought is discussed in the author's work: Michael Oppenheim, *Mutual Upholding: Fashioning Jewish Philosophy Through Letters* (New York: Peter Lang, 1992). Additionally, although I have not pursued the question here, in exploring the differences between the presentations of Davis and Levinas, the prominence of visual as against aural metaphors might be a fertile area. The possibility that there is a distinct difference in the use of these metaphors suggests itself because of Levinas's pervasive critique of the place of visual metaphors in traditional Western philosophy.

73   Levinas, *Totality*, 227.

Six

Charles Davis and the "Warm Current" of Critical Theology: A Feminist Critical Appreciation

MARSHA A. HEWITT

In the Introduction to his book *What Is Living, What Is Dead in Christianity Today?*, Charles Davis speaks of "the bold character of feminist theology," citing Terry Eagleton's assessment of feminist criticism as a "paradigm" of revolutionary criticism.[1] For Davis, feminist theology thus understood signals a "decisive break with the conformism of received theology,"[2] notwith-standing "the limitations of [its] present achievement."[3] Davis agrees with Eagleton's description of the features of revolutionary criticism insofar as they offer a model for the way in which "a critical theology can relate itself to emancipatory practice." In part, critical theology "must dismantle the ruling concepts of religion, reinserting religious texts into the whole field of cultural practices. It should articulate its cultural analyses with a consistent political intervention. It must engage with the language and the unconscious of religious texts, to reveal their role in the ideological construction of the subject." Furthermore, an analysis of the ideological function of religious texts (including religious traditions) must be oriented to the "transformation of the subject within a wider political context."[4]

Although Davis does not pursue the connection between critical theology and feminist theology, aspects of his thought nonetheless bear strong affinities with it. Feminist theology *is* a critical theology, in that it too aspires to similar goals outlined by Davis. Davis and some feminist theologians share as well a committed interest in exploring the possibilities for genuine intersubjectivity that necessarily involves social and personal transformation; in formulating a critique of domination as it exists within Christian theological discourse and practices; in reclaiming bodily, emotional, and sensuous experience within religious life, as well as affirming the struggle for social justice grounded in the individual and community's apprehension of Ultimate Reality, or Being.

With respect to these and other themes, the critical theology of many feminist writers and Davis expresses a utopian dimension best described in the words of Max Horkheimer as "the longing for the wholly Other" (*Die Sehnsucht nach dem ganz Anderen*).[5] One feminist critical theorist has described this longing as the "regulative principle of hope,"[6] without which radical transformation is unthinkable. As such, the longing for the wholly Other (which is an entirely religious longing) is a demand for justice and human well-being, for soul in soulless conditions, and the assurance that the murderer and the torturer do not have the last word. A critical theology of this kind attempts to retrieve the "warm current"[7] of the Christian religion (as distinct from elaborating the propositional content of theological doctrines), and emphasizes its intuitional core as the expression of unconditional love and openness toward both the transcendent and the human other.

Davis's appropriation of critical social theory, however, constitutes the real point of intersection between his critical theology and feminism.[8] Several themes addressed by critical theory and taken up by Davis also resonate throughout the work of some feminist theologians in a variety of ways. In discussing those themes in critical theory that appear in Davis and in feminist theology, I will show how Davis's notion of a critical theology contributes toward and may be enhanced by a feminist perspective. I take up this task with a view to situating Davis and feminist theology in terms of a dialectical and interpretive encounter whose aim is to foster a deeper critical awareness of the transformative potential of a socially and politically mediated religious consciousness and praxis.

I

Toward the end of *Theology and Political Society*, Davis describes "the mystical element in religion" as "the experience and subsequent conviction that at its deepest core the reality of my individual self becomes one with Ultimate Reality." This "mystical element" is "eminently political in as much as it is the deepest source and ground of politics. In releasing human persons into individual freedom as subjects, it makes possible the process of communication among free and equal participants, which is the essence of emancipated politics." The participants required to enact this form of emancipated politics must be human subjects structured around a "transcendent and indefeasibly private core."[9] Without the existence of such individuals, Davis warns, it is difficult to see "why the individual as a social factor should not be abolished as an obsolete historical form."[10]

This concern for the human individual and the preservation of her/his inner integrity is shared by the main representatives of Critical Theory, from Horkheimer through to Habermas, although conceptualized in different ways. For Horkheimer and Theodor Adorno, this concern was articulated both in terms of the dialectic of self-sacrifice and self-preservation in the emergence of the modern autonomous subject, and in exposing the illusory nature of individuality within mass culture.[11] The more hopeful utopian social philosophy of Herbert Marcuse envisioned the possibility of individuals committed to "the Great Refusal," who could resist the repressive power of the status quo through the release of psychic Eros which would restore to human beings the unalienated desire for joy, happiness, love and the capacity for sensuous receptivity experienced as conscious needs.[12] There are strong reverberations of Marcusian themes in Davis's affirmation of "feeling," "bodily reality" and "sensuousness," and the importance of eros in all dimensions of human experience.[13] Davis writes that "Feelings are the *eros* of our being when that being is aroused by its interaction with the reality of the other," and that "Underlying . . . the entirety of our interaction with the world around us is an *eros* or basic desire. That desire penetrates all our actions and determines the fundamental orientation of our embodied mind and spirit."[14]

What is interesting is that while these themes in Davis's work resonate with the utopian vision found in writers such as Marcuse, Davis's reception of critical theory into his critical theology comes largely by way of the discourse theory of Jürgen Habermas. Habermas's subject is a discursive agent who enters into free and unconstrained argumentation with other similarly constituted discursive individuals in order to establish those norms and normative institutional arrangements which all the participants recognize by consensus as valid for them. In this way, reciprocal, morally binding decisions are arrived at. Communicative action offers a *procedure* for dealing with validity claims and competing world views through which competent speakers may reclaim the integrity of their "lifeworld," thereby reversing the colonization of the lifeworld by the technical, instrumental rationality that defines the logic of the "system."[15]

Habermas's notion of the ideal speech community involves noncoercive and symmetrical relations of intersubjectivity where the only force permitted is the force of the better argument. In the model of community as discursively structured, what is pursued is mutual understanding achieved through a process of critical scrutiny of all values, norms and worldviews: "valid norms must be capable in principle of meeting with the rationally motivated approval of everyone affected under conditions that neutralize all motives except that of cooperatively seeking the truth."[16] Davis describes the concept of ideal speech as implying a "society free from domination, organized on a principle of equality and embodying the ideals of truth, freedom and justice."[17]

An important question arising out of discourse theory is: who are the participants, and what conditions are required that mediate their consciousness as individuals engaged in "free communication"[18] that Davis identifies with the "essence of emancipated politics?" How do these individuals come into being? Certainly, the level of self-awareness required of active participants in the discursive situation exists in varying degrees among the participants themselves which, in turn, affects their capacity to be active members of discourse activity at all. The existence of competent speakers presupposes a fairly well-developed sense of self-conscious individuality that is inevitably linked to gender formation and roles in a given society. A consideration of the problematics associated with women's struggles toward selfhood and autonomous individuality requires that communicative action theory include a feminist critique, especially as the latter concerns women's exclusion from the public realm and their historical condition of being silenced or not seriously listened to.[19] Without an analysis of the "interior self" that is attentive to gender and its central role in the formation of self-consciousness, the concept of such a self as the basis of the possibility of individual freedom is endangered by abstraction and disconnectedness with social reality.

To elaborate my point I turn to feminist critical theorist Seyla Benhabib's differentiation of the "generalized and the concrete other," with reference to modern ethical theory.[20] In brief, the perspective of the generalized other corresponds to the domain of moral theory that is concerned with the clarification and justification of principles and rights at the metaethical level of analysis. Its normative discourses focus on justice in the public, legal and legislative realms. The generalized other represents a moral universalism that is "*substitutionalist*, in the sense that the universalism [it] defend[s] is defined surreptitiously by identifying the experiences of a specific group of subjects as the paradigmatic case of the human as such. These subjects are invariably white, male adults who are propertied or at least professional."[21] In this tradition, the moral self is viewed as a "*disembedded* and *disembodied* being" whose vision of justice does not include needs associated with the realm of feeling and sensuousness as legitimate subjects of moral discourse.

Benhabib contrasts the moral point of view of the generalized other with that of the concrete other, whose moral perspective "requires us to view each and every rational being as an individual with a particular history, identity, and affective-emotional constitution."[22] The standpoint of the concrete other seeks to understand "the distinctiveness of the other . . . [in an effort] to comprehend the needs of the other, their motivations" and their desires.[23] The concept of intersubjectivity embraced by this moral point of view seeks to sustain and affirm difference and particularity, confirming not only the humanity of the other, but her/his "human *individuality*." The moral relations that accompany this kind of interaction belong most appropriately to what has become known in feminist literature as "an ethics of care and responsibility."[24]

For Benhabib, an account of the different moral perspectives of the generalized and the concrete other must consider the gendered features of both in order to illuminate the political implications of a moral theory that privileges one at the expense of the other. It also casts light on the notion of self that informs each moral point of view. The concept of self that corresponds to the generalized other assumes the male to be the legitimate moral agent who legislates justice in the public realm and who represents the perspective of a false universalism—false, because it excludes gender relations and their political implications from the sphere of justice by relegating them to the privatized realm of nature. "The sphere of justice from Hobbes through Locke and Kant is regarded as the domain where independent, male heads of household transact with one another, while the domestic-intimate sphere is put beyond the pale of justice and restricted to the reproductive and affective needs of the bourgeois paterfamilias. . . . An entire domain of human activity, namely, nurture, reproduction, love and care, which becomes the woman's lot in the course of the development of modern, bourgeois society, is excluded from moral and political considerations, and relegated to the real of 'nature.' "[25]

Benhabib criticizes Habermas for not adequately thematizing the standpoint of the concrete other, charging that his theory takes the generalized other to represent the moral point of view.[26] While Habermas's ethical theory may be recast to develop its latent possibilities for the articulation of the moral perspective of the concrete other, it nonetheless reproduces the Western tradition of silencing it. Perhaps this is due partly to the fact that, following Agnes Heller's critique of Habermas (also cited by Davis[27]), his theory is undermined by the absence of an historical subject, or "addressee": "The fact that he never had in mind a particular addressee has spared him the effort of formulating a theory which would be appropriate to its possible reception." Heller also claims that "Habermasian man has . . . no body, no feelings; the 'structure of personality' is identified with cognition, language and interaction."[28] If the subject of Habermas's discursive communities has neither body nor feelings, then the mutual understanding to which it strives in communicative interaction with others amounts to little more than the activity of "fictitiously defined selves"[29] who displace what ought to be the focus on concrete, embodied selves striving for autonomy and mutual recognition of their needs and desires.

Benhabib, however, does not advocate replacing the moral point of view of the generalized other with that of the concrete other, but rather attempts to correct what she sees as the exclusivist emphasis of the former, so that *both* perspectives of the generalized and concrete other may be recognized as mutually enhancing and interdependent. Benhabib seeks to expand the object domain of moral discourse to include rights *and* needs, recognizing that discourse on matters of justice and rights alone is empty and abstract unless rooted in a vision of the good life, defined in an open-ended way through ongoing moral conversations about the kind of existence that can promote the satisfaction of the whole community's desires for happiness, pleasure, and freedom. Here we see a resurfacing of the Marcusian preoccupation with social transformation geared to producing conditions which allow for the meeting of genuine human needs. In order to bring the moral perspectives of the generalized and concrete other into a dialectical tension with each other, it is necessary to conceptualize intersubjectivity within a more fully articulated theory and politics of difference.

II

Feminist theology is turning its attention increasingly toward formulating more complex theories of difference, as well as toward interrogating current feminist assumptions of a universal female subject in whom all concrete differences among individual women may be ultimately reconciled. The theme of a universal female subject has been recently criticized by Elisabeth Schüssler Fiorenza as representing "the totalizing discourse of Western universalist feminism"[30] which privileges a logic of identity over difference in presupposing an ontologically based correspondence between the subject of feminist discourse, "woman," and all individual women. Many feminist theorists are calling for a radical rethinking of the "ontological constructions of identity"[31] in order to more adequately understand how social systems of power produce and reproduce the very subjects they represent.

If women are to be released from the category of the "unitary otherness" of man, which itself perpetuates the classic gender-dualism and polarity of Western philosophical and theological discourses, then feminist discourses "must engage at one and the same time in a continuing critical deconstruction of the politics of otherness, in reclaiming and reconstructing our particular experiences, histories, and identities, as well as in sustaining a permanent reflection on our common differences."[32] Part of this task involves the critical articulation of the way in which subjectivity is "discursively constituted by the very political system that is supposed to facilitate its emancipation. . . . It is not enough to enquire into how women might become more fully represented in language and politics [or theology]. Feminist critique ought also to understand how the category of 'women,' the subject of feminism, is produced and restrained by the very structures of power through which emancipation is sought."[33]

Davis's concept of the "interior self" needs to include an account of the formation of the human individual that recognizes how selves become discursively produced in *different* ways by the prevailing power structures of a given socio-political order. Davis's dialectic of the interior self as an "individuated person" who becomes so through "political relationships with others," thereby creating the very possibility of political action,[34] anticipates the feminist account of identity described above. What Davis does not sufficiently emphasize is the necessity of historical struggle against oppressive power structures as a key element in the formation of the self-conscious political subject. According to Schüssler Fiorenza, the 'option for the oppressed' is an '*option for ourselves.*' Self-identity *as women* cannot be assumed but must be chosen in the commitment to the struggle for ending patriarchal structures of oppression. Moreover, the 'politics of otherness' can be displaced only when identity is no longer articulated as unitary universal identity and established either by exclusion and domination of the others or by the other's self-negation and subordination."[35]

The notion of the "interior self " as a necessary condition of an emancipated politics may be strengthened through a more expansive elaboration of the conditions of its own possibility, which in turn requires a theory of nonidentity and difference that resists absorption by categories of "unitary universal identity" which are not only elusive and abstract, but also function as regulatory mechanisms of domination. Certainly, Habermas's model of discursive communities whose members are engaged in a free and open process of seeking mutual understanding falls short of a theory of intersubjectivity that consciously embraces and sustains difference and contradiction. To this end, the negative dialectics of Theodor Adorno, whatever its difficulties, is more promising.[36]

Adorno defined negative dialectics as "the consistent sense of non-identity."[37] He developed his theory as a critique of the totalizing philosophical system of Hegel, proclaiming in a reversal of Hegel, that "The whole is the false."[38] For Adorno, Western philosophical traditions are predicated upon the principle of identity—"the primal form of ideology"[39]—which seeks to ensure that the object of thought is absorbed in the concept itself. The logic of identity operative in these totalizing systems enact a philosophical imperialism of "annexing the alien,"[40] obliterating all difference, designating that which resists the colonization of the concept as despised contradiction, the presence of "non-identity under the aspect of identity."[41] The preservation of the subject requires that dialectics attempt not to resolve contradiction in a false reconciliation that "perpetuates antagonism by suppressing contradiction,"[42] but rather to let the other be, and to be near it in allowing it to remain "distant and different, beyond the heterogeneous and beyond that which is one's own."[43] Utopia would then be "above identity and above contradiction; it would be a togetherness of diversity."[44]

One of the ways of "rescuing" things from the violence of the insatiable identity principle—which for Adorno, is an act of love—is through memory, that is, the memory of suffering. In the memory of suffering lies the history of human and nonhuman nature (*Leidensgeschichte*) and their possible redemption: "The need to lend a voice to suffering is a condition of all truth."[45] The theme of the redemptive power of memory is shared by Davis and some feminist theologians in a way that situates them closely to Adorno and Walter Benjamin. For Benjamin, historical memory is intertwined with the hope that the slaughtered innocents of the past did not perish for nothing, and that the memory of their concrete struggles and sufferings might be translated into a political motivation for change. Like the "Angel of History" in his famous "Theses on the Philosophy of History,"[46] Benjamin looks backward to history rather than forward, surveying "the destruction of material nature as it *has actually taken place.*"[47] A sustained recollection of the real sufferings of past epochs allows for a conceptualization of the future world of the "not-yet" that condemns past wrongs while promising the fulfillment of past hopes. Thus for Benjamin, the "theological illumination that redeems past history, and political education that condemns it, are one and the same endeavour."[48]

Davis shares a similar focus on history as the recollection of the sufferings of past victims, taking up the theme of "anamnestic solidarity," a solidarity-in-remembrance with the dead that infuses the present. He invokes Christian Lenhardt's argument that the present generations which benefit from past struggles must honour those struggles in memory, insisting that "the unity of repressed mankind is the solidarity of the living with the dead."[49] Without this solidarity forged in remembrance, the struggles of past generations for liberation are appropriated by present generations in an instrumental fashion, resulting in a materially better-off society whose members lack heart. The exploited victims of the past would then be exploited again in an opportunistic appropriation of their misery and sacrifice. In memory of them, present generations may become inspired to work for changing conditions that produce the suffering of the innocents, rendering the past as never finished, but working within the present toward the realization of a better future. In the often-quoted words of Walter Benjamin, it is "Only for the sake of the hopeless are we given hope."[50]

Memory of the past sufferings of women emerges as an empowering theme in feminist theology in a way that deepens the notion of anamnestic solidarity[51] by giving voice to the actual lived sufferings of women and their struggles against the oppressive conditions of patriarchal power. Elisabeth Schüssler Fiorenza's reconstruction of early Christian history reveals not only how women suffered, but also their vital role in the development and preservation of Christianity. This reclamation and articulation of the sacrifices and struggles of women in past epochs functions subversively as a "dangerous memory" which threatens to shatter the alienation and injustice of the existent. "We participate in the same struggle as our biblical foresisters against the oppression of patriarchy and for survival and freedom from it. We share the same liberating visions and commitments as our biblical foremothers. We are not called to 'empathize' or 'identify' with *their* struggles and hopes but to continue *our* struggle in solidarity with them."[52] Schüssler Fiorenza focuses on the individual stories of past women and their liberating, prophetic actions, such as the woman who anointed Jesus, in a way that both preserves and sustains their particularity as well as animating present struggles for the liberation of women. The woman who anointed Jesus was ridiculed and humiliated for her action which Jesus acknowledged as a prophetic recognition of who he was. It is "a politically dangerous story."[53]

The importance of memory as an act of *solidarity-in-remembrance* informs women's present experience, becoming part of their critical consciousness in the contemporary struggle for liberation. Rosemary Radford Ruether (whom Davis associates with "the bold character of feminist theology"), describes the "uniqueness of feminist theology" as residing in the focus not merely on experience, but on *women's* experience "which has been almost entirely shut out of theological reflection in the past."[54] She locates the "critical principle" of feminist theology in the struggle for "the promotion of the full humanity of women"[55] which releases the voices of women historically marginalized and silenced because of the inability (or refusal) of the theological tradition to accept their full humanity. That which in the Christian tradition "denies" or "distorts" women's full humanity Ruether appraises "as not redemptive" and inauthentic: the negation of the prophetic, emancipatory current within Christianity. In claiming the critical principle of full humanity normatively ascribed to men for themselves as well, women begin to realize their subjectivity and their legitimate participation in proclaiming "the authentic message of redemption and the mission of the redemptive community."[56]

For both Schüssler Fiorenza and Ruether, the notion of community as a kind of renewed prophetic "Church" is vital to the struggles of women for full liberation. Schüssler Fiorenza's idea of the "*ekklesia*" of women, or women-Church, is a dialogical community that resonates with the Habermasian model of discursive communities, providing a place where women engage in an ongoing discussion of values and norms as well as sharing of experiences and hopes in a process of decision-making about their own "spiritual-political" and "theological religious" affairs.[57] The *ekklesia* of women offers the experience of free interaction oriented to seeking out ever renewed possibilities for authentic intersubjectivity. In this way, women can acknowledge and affirm each other's difference as they engage in a shared struggle toward personal and social transformation. Such communities are constituted not by formal membership, but in and through relationships which recognize in faithful memory of early Christian communities that the presence of God is experienced "among one another and through one another."[58] The *ekklesia* of women is the locus of divine revelation and the nurturing grace that empowers and grounds the struggle for liberation.

Ruether embraces a similar notion of community whereby women and men are converted to reciprocal relationality as a way of life; who seek to overcome the polarizations and antagonisms of gender differences. She envisions a "conversion to community"[59] that negates the alienation and distortions of relationships that foster domination and exploitation. In similar fashion to Davis, Ruether understands that such communities are constituted by "grounded," "relational" selves who relate to each other in and through mutual service. Ruether calls for the transformation of Church into "liberation community,"[60] where men enter into a real solidarity with women in striving for a multidimensional liberation which recognizes that "the struggle against sexism is basically a struggle to humanize the world, to humanize ourselves, to salvage the planet, to be in right relation to God/ess. At this point, men and women really join hands in a common struggle."[61]

III

For both Schüssler Fiorenza and Ruether, the struggle against the oppression of women that is forged in memory of past injustices and real sufferings is one that also seeks the liberation of all human beings. "Women-identified men" are also engaged in a process of self-transformation away from sexism. Together with women, they form liberation communities rooted in the moral and political perspective of the concrete other, without whose liberation an emancipated society is not possible.

These practical discursive communities critically nuance Davis's stress on consensus and unity as the presupposition of communicative action. According to Davis, consensus inheres within pluralism: "A pluralist society . . . presupposes a consensus, created and maintained freely in open discussion. A public consensus will not eliminate dissent; indeed, as a freely created agreement it presupposes and implies dissent. But dissent is identified as dissent *with reference to the consensus, and a minimum of consensus is a condition for political argument*."[62]

The kind of discursive communities implied by Schüssler Fiorenza and Ruether shift the emphasis away from *consensus* to the dialogical *process* itself as an ongoing moral conversation that infuses daily life and presupposes relationships of universal respect and egalitarian reciprocity. The expansion of the discursive situation to include a sustained and continuous discussion of the needs and aspirations of particular groups and individuals allows for the greater visibility of the other's point of view and the distinctiveness of her/his reality. Thus, we need to privilege the discursive *process* over consensus as a commitment to a way of life that is critically self-reflective and open to change as new conversation partners enter the discursive field, bringing with them new articulations of need and desire. In this way, critical discourse theory pledges itself to a radical democratization of its own procedures so that points of view that are routinely invisible due to historical repression and social marginalization find expression. Refined in this way, discourse ethics proceeds from the recognition that the "moral imagination involves representative thinking, namely, the capacity to take the standpoint of others involved into account and to reason from their point of view."[63]

There are other important themes elaborated in both feminist theology and critical theory that are also present in the critical theology of Davis, if not as explicitly developed. While Davis defines tradition as "the ground of values, not as an external or heteronomous authority, but as their real presence in history,"[64] he is also aware that this history is not entirely innocent. Thus, the task of a critical theology must include a critique of tradition insofar as religion and theology function as "instances of domination."[65] Much feminist theology arises out of this awareness, setting itself the critical task of exposing those "instances of domination" that have rendered and continue to render women as subjugated and inferior within the Christian tradition. Feminist critical theology both deconstructs and reconstructs tradition in an effort to discover what is genuinely redemptive and liberating in it for women, and what is to be discarded as inauthentic and repressive, thereby negating God's saving grace. In this sense, feminist critical theology concurs with Davis's assertion that "Faith comes to us as the personal appropriation of the collective remembrance of a community, a remembrance that has accumulated a long historical experience, together with many attempts at its expression."[66]

At the same time, feminist critical theology goes somewhat further than this insofar as it is connected with a historical and political movement for the liberation of women. This movement, whether it finds expression in various types of "women-Church" or other forms of liberation communities, privileges experience to a degree that Davis does not. Again, I turn to Schüssler Fiorenza and Ruether for an elaboration of women's experience as the source of authentic theological reflection and liberating political praxis. According to Sheila Greeve Davaney, both Schüssler Fiorenza and Ruether claim that "feminist experience and norms are grounded in the encounter with the divine and that such encounter gives them a validity, a 'true' quality, that the experiences and criteria of the 'false and alienated' world of patriarchy do not have. For both theologians, the liberating God or God/ess is both the foundation of women's critical experience and the source of its validation."[67]

Davaney objects to what she sees as an implicit claim in Schüssler Fiorenza and Ruether's view of the nature of women's experience, as giving women a "privileged access to the realm of the ontologically real" which simultaneously contradicts their professed understanding of the social character of experience.[68] In other words, one cannot justifiably advance a theory that lays claim to both historical adequacy and ontological validity. As Davaney sees it, no point of view, no matter how critical, can reveal "the way things really are" since "all we have are alternative ways of conceiving reality."[69] While I am not prepared at this point to debate the merits of Davaney's criticism as it applies to these feminist theologians, there is a great deal of validity in her general cautioning against ontologizing *any* particular experience, as such a move inevitably will be at the expense of others. This results in a reassertion of the logic of identity that represses difference and diversity for the sake of its own drive toward unity. Feminism cannot advocate or assume a commonality of female experience and remain a critical theory and practice of liberation because to do so results in the suppression—however unintentional—of the very real differences between women, such as class, race, education, culture and language. A feminist critique that overprivileges women's experience in the way criticized by

Davaney restores the hegemony of the moral perspective of the generalized other.[70]

Davaney's critique of the tendency to ontologize women's experience by claiming it as "the source for theological reflection and the norm for evaluating the adequacy of any theological framework"[71] does not (and ought not) compromise the necessity of exposing the actual human suffering and struggle of any historical group as "the condition of all truth," however. Davaney ends her article by offering an alternative concept of experience that preserves its critical function by maintaining it as discursively constituted and assessed in light of the pragmatic norms to which it gives rise in a way that sustains particularity without privileging any specific point of view. Davaney is close to Habermas in her rejection of ontological foundations as providing an adequate basis for evaluating norms and moral decisions. Along with Davis, she too locates political action in "participation in the social conversation and the public evaluation of what should count as desirable consequences."[72] However, she departs from Davis's view of the ontological grounding of discourse by insisting on the thoroughly "historical and conflictual character of experience." Davaney further repudiates any kind of referential interpretation of religious symbols in favour of a view that recognizes all religious symbolism as "human constructions" whose " 'truth' . . . lies not in how well they depict some ontological structure of reality, but in the forms of experience engendered by commitment to such values."[73] Davaney relocates the locus of women's experience away from any concept of universal experience or grounding in divine reality, as part of a necessary move in the emancipatory interest of preserving the particularity of women in all their social and historical diversity.

Although Davis rejects interpretations of Christian symbols as offering an "objectively validated account in propositional form of God, the cosmos, human life and history,"[74] he would nonetheless disagree with Davaney's conclusion on the grounds that she sacrifices the very basis upon which the human subject as political actor is at all possible. As indicated earlier, surely the very possibility of the interior self as described by Davis is predicated upon certain historical experiences and cultural conditions that could inhibit or even preclude individual formation. Here I have in mind Davis's own critique of Habermas which cautions that freedom cannot be struggled for only in speech acts, and that ideal discourse requires an ideal social situation as a condition of its possibility. Davis tells us, and rightly, that freedom is a "social and cumulative experience," "preserved and transmitted" through tradition.[75] But what if that very tradition has been so repressive and dominating to some groups and individuals as to severely undermine the development of an individuated self at all? Would not a corresponding religious consciousness reflect an alienated sense of relationship with God that could not be overcome unless and until historical conditions are transformed so that human beings *as human* may come into being?

IV

Davis's critical theology is implicitly open to addressing these questions, but will not be able to go further without including a fuller account of the historically situated perspective of the concrete other. It is here that a feminist critique has much to offer, in that it too participates in the emancipatory project of critical theology. At the same time, Davis's understanding of Christian identity contributes to feminism by compelling us to envision possibilities of forming communities that avoid the pitfalls of overprivileging a particular experience, and where difference and otherness are not rendered invisible through exclusion, but are rather embraced as mutually enriching and enhancing for all individuals. His is also a profoundly ecumenical vision in its acknowledgement of the validity of all the world's religions. "Christian identity," he writes, "is not grounded upon membership in a particular Church" but is one "mode or manifestation of a more fundamental religious identity, which we share with people from other religious traditions, as all being participates in a single total history."[76] Such a notion of religious identity and human community is deeply feminist in spirit, forged in the loving capacity to see the world as it might present itself from the standpoint of redemption, illuminated by a truly Messianic light.

Notes

1   Terry Eagleton, *Walter Benjamin or Towards a Revolutionary Criticism* (London: Verso, 1981), 98, cited in Charles Davis, *What Is Living, What Is Dead in Christianity Today?* (San Francisco: Harper & Row, 1986).

2   Davis, *What Is Living*, 4.

3 Davis does not quote Eagleton's elaboration of the deficiencies of feminist criticism, which claim, among other things, that the promise of feminist theory remain on the level of "intention" as opposed to "achievement." But Eagleton's real dispute with feminism concerns the sectarian, separatist tendencies of "radical feminism" that Eagleton identifies with "petty-bourgeois ideology." For the full text of his argument, see *Walter Benjamin* (98-100). Davis's reference to the "limitations of [the] present achievement" of feminist theology in the context of his discussion of Eagleton may be interpreted to show a basic agreement with Eagleton's reservations, although Davis himself does not articulate what his own reservations are. That Davis agrees in general with Eagleton on this point may be further argued given Davis's reference to Rosemary Radford Ruether as an example of the "bold character" of feminist theology. Her work is highly critical of separatist-exclusivist forms of feminist theology.

4 Davis, *What Is Living*, 4.

5 Max Horkheimer, *Die Sehnsucht nach dem ganz Anderen, Ein Interview mit Kommentar von Helmut Gumnior* (Hamburg: Furche-Verlag, 1970).

6 Seyla Benhabib, "Feminism and Postmodernism: An Uneasy Alliance," *Praxis International* 11, no.2 (July 1991): 147.

7 See Russel Jacoby's reference to Ernst Bloch's description of the "warm current" of Marxism, in *Dialectic of Defeat: Contours of Western Marxism* (Cambridge: Cambridge University Press, 1981), 34.

8 My use of the term "feminism" is inclusive of both feminist theology and feminist nontheological theory; indeed, feminist theology is a feminist theory.

9 Charles Davis, *Theology and Political Society* (Cambridge: Cambridge University Press, 1980), 180.

10 Ibid., 181.

11 See Max Horkheimer and Theodor W. Adorno, *Dialectic of Enlightenment*, trans. John Cumming (New York: The Seabury Press, 1972); especially "Excursus 1," 43-80, and "The Culture Industry," 120-67.

12 Herbert Marcuse, *Eros and Civilization: A Philosophical Enquiry into Freud* (New York: Vintage Books, 1962), and "Marxism and Feminism," *Women's Studies* 2 (1974): 279-88.

13 Charles Davis, *Body as Spirit: The Nature of Religious Feeling* (New York: The Seabury Press, 1976).

14 Charles Davis, "*Eros* and Objective Reason," *Journal of Religion and Culture* (Spring 1991): 46.

15 For a complete discussion of what Habermas means by "lifeworld" and "system" and how they are differentiated, see his *The Theory of Communicative Action*, Vol. 2, trans. Thomas McCarthy (Boston: Beacon Press, 1987).

16 Jürgen Habermas, *The Theory of Communication Action*, Vol. 1, trans. Thomas McCarthy (Boston: Beacon Press, 1984), 19.

17 Davis, *Theology and Political Society*, 94.

18 Ibid., 178.

19 I have discussed this problem at greater length in my article, "The Politics of Empowerment: Ethical Paradigms in a Feminist Critique of Critical Social Theory," *The Annual of the Society of Christian Ethics* (1990): 184-87.

20 Seyla Benhabib, "The Generalized and the Concrete Other," in Seyla Benhabib and Drucilla Cornell, eds., *Feminism as Critique: On the Politics of Gender* (Minneapolis: University of Minnesota Press), 77-95; and Seyla Benhabib, *Critique, Norm, and Utopia: A Study of the Foundations of Critical Theory* (New York: Columbia University Press, 1986).

21 Benhabib, "Generalized and Concrete Other," 86.

22 Benhabib, *Critique, Norm, and Utopia*, 341.

23 Ibid.

24 See Carol Gilligan, *In a Different Voice: Psychological Theory and Women's Development* (Cambridge, MA: Harvard University Press, 1982), for the best known and perhaps most debated elaboration of the ethics of care and responsibility.

25 Benhabib, "Generalized and Concrete Other," 83.

26 Benhabib, *Critique, Norm, and Utopia*, 339.

27 Charles Davis, "Kommunikative Rationalität und die Grundlegung christlicher Hoffnung," in Edmund Arens, ed., *Habermas und die Theologie: Bieträge zur theologischen Rezeption, Diskussion und Kritik der Theorie kommunikativen Handelns* (Düsseldorf: Patmos, 1989), 97-98. An English version of this essay can be found in Charles Davis, *Religion and the Making of Society: Essays in Social Theology* (Cambridge: Cambridge University Press, 1994), 188-205.

28 Agnes Heller, "Habermas and Marxism," in John B. Thompson and David Held, eds., *Habermas: Critical Debates* (Cambridge, MA: MIT Press, 1982), 21, 22.

29 Benhabib, "Generalized and Concrete Other," 81.

30 Elisabeth Schüssler Fiorenza, "The Politics of Otherness: Biblical Interpretation as a Critical Praxis for Liberation," in Marc H. Ellis and Otta Maduro, eds., *The Future of Liberation Theology: Essays in Honor of Gustavo Gutierrez* (Maryknoll: Orbis Books, 1989), 316.

31 Judith Butler, *Gender Trouble: Feminism and the Subversion of Identity* (New York: Routledge, 1990), 5.

32 Schüssler Fiorenza, "Politics of Otherness," 316, 317.

33 Butler, *Gender Trouble*, 2.

34 Davis, *Theology and Political Society*, 178.

35 Schüssler Fiorenza, "Politics of Otherness," 317-18.

36 In *Theology and Political Society*, Davis criticizes Adorno's "refusal to affirm explicitly" the moral position that grounds his negative dialects as "unstable and inconsistent in its functioning" (138). However, Adorno was acutely aware of the way in which stable theories tend to become ideological and repressive, thereby doing violence to their objects. His "inconsistency" and "instability" in this sense is consciously sustained.

37   Theodor W. Adorno, *Negative Dialectics*, trans. E.B. Ashton (New York: Continuum, 1973), 5.

38   Theodor W. Adorno, *Minima Moralia: Reflections from Damaged Life*, trans. E.F.N. Jephcott (London: Verso, 1985), 50.

39   Ibid., 148.

40   Ibid., 191.

41   Ibid., 5.

42   Ibid., 142.

43   Ibid., 191.

44   Ibid., 150.

45   Ibid., 17.

46   Walter Benjamin, *Illuminations*, trans. Harry Zohn and ed. Hannah Arendt (New York: Schocken Books, 1969). For a moving and insightful interpretation of the "Theses," see Charles Davis, "Walter Benjamin: The Mystical Materialist," in Howard Joseph, Jack N. Lightstone, and Michael D. Oppenheim, eds., *Truth and Compassion: Essays on Judaism and Religion in Memory of Dr. Solomon Frank* (Waterloo: Wilfrid Laurier University Press, 1983).

47   Susan Buck-Morss, *The Dialectics of Seeing: Walter Benjamin and the Arcades Project* (Cambridge, MA: The MIT Press, 1989), 95.

48   Ibid., 245.

49   In Davis, *Theology and Political Society*, 145.

50   Quoted in Theodor W. Adorno, *Prisms*, trans. Samuel and Shierry Weber (Cambridge, MA: The MIT Press, 1990), 241. Also quoted at the end of Herbert Marcuse's *One-Dimensional Man: Studies in the Ideology of Advanced Industrial Society* (Boston: Beacon Press, 1968), 257.

51   The category of "suffering humanity" is insufficient and abstract unless the suffering and injustice experienced by specific groups and individuals is made visible. People suffer more or less, and in different ways than others, and unless these differences and degrees are explicated, we are left with a vague and politically impotent concept of human suffering. Focusing on the suffering of a particular group, such as women, allows us to penetrate the actual dynamics of oppression, which further allows for a deeper understanding of the suffering resulting from racial and class oppression, for example.

52   Elisabeth Schüssler Fiorenza, *Bread Not Stone: The Challenge of Feminist Biblical Interpretation* (Boston: Beacon Press, 1984), 5.

53   Elisabeth Schüssler Fiorenza, *In Memory of Her: A Feminist Reconstruction of Christian Origins* (New York: Crossroad, 1984), xiv.

54   Rosemary Radford Ruether, *Sexism and God-Talk: Toward a Feminist Theology* (Boston: Beacon Press, 1983), 13.

55   Ibid., 18.

56   Ibid., 18, 19.

57   Schüssler Fiorenza, *In Memory of Her*, 344.

58   Ibid., 345.

59   Ruether, *Sexism and God Talk*, 164.

60   Ibid., 202.

61   Ibid., 191-92.

62   Charles Davis, "The Philosophical Foundations of Pluralism," in I. Beaubien, Charles Davis, and Gilles Langevin, eds., *Le Pluralisme: Symposium interdisciplinaire/ Pluralism: Its Meaning Today* (Montréal: Fides, 1974), 247 (italics added). Also cited in *Theology and Political Society*, 169.

63   Seyla Benhabib, "Afterword: Communicative Ethics and Contemporary Controversies in Practical Philosophy," in Seyla Benhabib and Fred Dallmayr, eds., *The Communicative Ethics Controversy* (Cambridge, MA: The MIT Press, 1990), 362.

64   Davis, *Theology and Political Society*, 96.

65   Ibid., 131.

66   Ibid., 151.

67   Sheila Greeve Davaney, "The Limits of the Appeal to Women's Experience," in Clarissa W. Atkinson, Constance H. Buchnan, and Margaret R. Miles, eds., *Shaping New Vision: Gender and Values in American Culture* (Ann Arbor and London: UMI Research Press, 1987), 37.

68   Ibid., 42.

69   Ibid., 43.

70   Perhaps Davaney has uncovered an antimony of feminist theory, which may be the inescapable result of any emancipatory theory committed to fully articulating the historical experiences and perspective of any specific subjugated group.

71   Ibid., 32.

72   Ibid., 47.

73   Ibid., 48.

74   Davis, *What Is Living*, 118. Davis explains the "objective reference" of religious "symbolic constructs" as "the reality of mystery," which is "beyond the ability of the subject to do more than affirm its presence" (115).

75   Davis, *Theology and Political Society*, 95-97.

76   Ibid., 170-71.

Charles Davis
A Selected Bibliography of His Work

Compiled by

DANIEL CERE

Books

A Question of Conscience. London: Hodder & Stoughton, 1967; New York: Harper & Row, 1967. Paperback edition, London: Hodder & Stoughton, 1969. French translation: *Une Question de Conscience.* Paris: Grasset, 1968. German translation: *Katholizismus heute?* Munchen: Nymphenberger Verlagshandlung, 1969. Dutch translation: *Omwille van het geweten.* Hilversum: Brand, 1968.

Christ and the World Religions. London: Hodder & Stoughton, 1970.

The Temptations of Religion. London: Hodder & Stoughton, 1973; revised edition, New York: Harper & Row, 1974.

Body as Spirit: The Nature of Religious Feeling. New York: Seabury Press, 1976; London: Hodder & Stoughton, 1977.

Theology and Political Society. Cambridge: Cambridge University Press, 1980.

What Is Living, What Is Dead In Christianity Today? Breaking the Liberal-Conservative Deadlock. San Francisco: Harper & Row, 1986.

Soft Bodies in a Hard World: Spirituality for the Vulnerable. Toronto: Anglican Book Centre, 1987.

Religion and the Making of Society: Essays in Social Theology. Cambridge, New York: Cambridge University Press, 1994.

Contributions to Books or Symposia

"Theology and Its Present Task." In *Theology and the University*, edited by John Coulson, 107-32. London: Darton, Longman & Todd, 1964; Baltimore: Helicon Press, 1964.

"The Philosophical Foundations of Pluralism." In *Le Pluralisme/Pluralism: Its Meaning Today*, edited by I. Beaubien, Charles Davis, Gilles Langevin, and Roger Lapointe, 223-50. Montréal: Fides, 1974.

"Introduction to the Philosophy Section." In *Le Pluralisme/Pluralism: Its Meaning Today*, edited by I. Beaubien, Charles Davis, Gilles Langevin, and Roger Lapointe, 219-22. Montréal: Fides, 1974.

"The Kingdom of Truth." In *The Upper Room Disciplines*, edited by Tom Page, 341-47. Nashville, TN: Upper Room, 1979.

"The Critical Function of the Concept of the Church in Nineteenth-Century Theology." In *Community and Critique in Nineteenth-Century Theology*, edited by Charles Davis, 7-22. Montréal: Interuniversity Centre for European Studies, 1980.

"The Experience of God and the Search for Images." In *Is God God?*, edited by A. Steuer and J.W. McClendon, 38-54. Nashville: Abingdon, 1981.

"Fluent Benthamites and Muddled Coleridgians: The Liberal and Conservative Traditions in Discourse." In *Papers of the 19th-Century Theology Working Group VII: AAR 1982 Meeting*, edited by Garrett Green and Marilyn Massey, 45-53. New York: Graduate Theological Union, 1982.

"Reason, Tradition, Community: The Search for Ethical Foundations." In *Foundations of Ethics*, edited by Leroy S. Rouner, 37-56. Notre Dame: University of Notre Dame Press, 1983.

"Walter Benjamin: The Mystical Materialist." In *Truth and Compassion: Essays on Judaism and Religion for Rabbi Solomon Frank*, edited by Howard Joseph, Jack N. Lightstone, and Michael D. Oppenheim, 75-89. Waterloo: Wilfrid Laurier University Press, 1983.

"Critical Theory." In *The Westminster Dictionary of Theology*, edited by Alan Richardson and John Bowden, 133-35. Philadelphia: Westminster Press, 1983.

"The Limits of Politics: The Christian Clash with Radicalism." In *Cities of Gods: Faith, Politics and Pluralism in Judaism, Christianity and Islam*, edited by Nigel Biggar, James S. Scott, and William Schweiker, 143-50. New York: Greenwood Press, 1986.

"Kommunikative Rationalität und die Grundlegung christlicher Hoffnung." In *Habermas und die Theologie*, edited by Edmund Arens, 96-114. Dusseldorf: Patmos Verlag, 1989.

"Pluralism, Privacy, and the Interior Self." In *Habermas, Modernity, and Public Theology*, edited by Don S. Browning and Francis Schüssler Fiorenza, 152-72. New York: Crossroad, 1992.

Articles

"Why I Left the Roman Catholic Church." *The Observer*, January 1, 1967, 21-22.

"Religious Pluralism and the New Counter-Culture." *The Listener*, April 9, 1970, 478-80.

"Küng on Infallibility." *Commonweal* 93 (1971): 445-47.

"Questions for the Papacy Today." *Concilium* 4, no.7 (1971): 12-20.

"Theological Method." *Theoria O Theory* 7 (1973): 50-53.

"Theology and Praxis." *Cross Currents* 23 (1973): 154-68.

"The Reconvergence of Theology and Religious Studies." *Studies in Religion/Sciences Religieuses* 4, no.3 (1974-75): 205-21.

"Religion and the Sense of the Sacred." *Catholic Theological Society Association Proceedings* 31 (1976): 85-107.

"The Christian Response to Secularization—History and Humanism: Essays in Honour of V.G. Kiernan." *New Edinburgh Review*, no. 38-39 (1977): 17-24.

"Is the Church an Idol?" *Commonweal* 107 (1980): 45-48.

"Our New Religious Identity." *Studies in Religion/Sciences Religieuses* 9 (1980): 25-39.

"Lonergan's Appropriation of the Concept of Praxis." *New Blackfriars* 62 (1981): 114-26.

"Theology and Religious Studies." *Scottish Journal of Religious Studies* 2 (1981): 11-20.

"The Theological Career of Historical Criticism of the Bible." *Cross Currents* 32 (1982): 267-84.

"Trois approches récentes dans l'étude des religions" (with M. Boutin and N. King). *Science et Esprit* 35 (1983): 325-51.

"The Church as a Structure of Communication." *Christian Understanding Everywhere*, no. 11 (1983): 11-15.

"Symposium on Religion and Politics." *Telos* 58 (1983-84): 129-30.

"Wherein There is No Ecstacy." *Studies in Religion/Sciences Religieuses* 13 (1984): 393-400.

"Learning to Say No to Nuclear War." *Arc* 13 (1985): 5-12.

"From Inwardness to Social Action: A Shift in the Locus of Religious Experience." *New Blackfriars* 67 (1986): 114-25.

"The Immanence of Knowledge and the Ecstacy of Faith." *Studies in Religion/Sciences Religieuses* 15 (1986): 191-96.

"Religion and the Making of Society." *Northwestern University Law Review* 81 (1987): 718-31.

"The End of Religion." *Compass* 6 (1988): 6-9.

"Is the Maleness of Jesus a Sacred Sign?" *Tablet* 243 (1989): 190-92.

"Death and the Sense of Ending." *Studies in Religion/Sciences Religieuses* 18 (1989): 51-60.

"Sacrifice and Violence: New Perspectives in the Theory of Religion from René Girard." *New Blackfriars* 70 (1989): 311-28.

"The Political Use and Misuse of Religious Language." *Journal of Ecumenical Studies* 26 (1989): 483-95.

"Our Modern Identity: The Formation of the Self." *Modern Theology* 6 (1990): 159-71.

"Eros and Objective Reason." *Journal of Religion and Culture* 5 (1991): 45-94.

"Charles Davis on Why it Was Not Enough to Ignore the Church." *National Catholic Reporter*, February 7, 1992, 14.

"Between Nihilism and Idolatry: Faith as the Non-experience of the Transcendent." *Lonergan Review* 1 (1992): 56-68.

Index

Adorno, Theodor, W., 2, 19, 26, 67, 119, 124, 132, 133, 134

Barth, Karl, 24
Baucom, Donald, 92
Baum, Gregory, 1
Beach, Steven, 92
Benhabib, Seyla, 25, 30, 31, 120-22, 132, 133, 135
Benjamin, Walter, 17, 34, 36-38, 47, 68, 125, 134
Bernstein, Richard, 26, 30
Blondel, Maurice, 28-29
Bottomore, Tom, 19
Brown, Scott, 91
Buber, Martin, 53, 113
Buck-Morss, Susan, 134
Butler, Judith, 133
Byrne, Partick, 90, 91

Carpenter, Susan, 91
Congar, Yves, 23
Coulson, John, 23
Cox, Harvey, 51, 53, 60
Crossan, John Domminic, 68, 113
Curran, Charles, E., 73

Daly, Mary, 35
Davaney, Sheila Greeve, 129-30
Davis, Charles, 17, 18, 19, 20, 21, 22, 34, 47, 48, 73, 74, 90, 91, 114, 115, 116,
    122, 123, 126, 127, 130, 132, 133, 134, 135
    and critical theology, 2, 3, 4, 11, 14-17, 41, 43-46, 62-63, 68, 69, 76, 89,
        117-18, 129, 131
    and critical theory, 3, 4, 13, 41, 58, 64-67, 69-70, 76-79, 82-86, 96, 118-20,
        125, 128
    and critique of religious orthodoxy, 12-14, 60
    and epistemology, 54-55, 60, 62, 71
    and modernity, 52-53, 60-61, 71
    and pluralism, 69, 75, 77-81, 93-100, 106-13
    and praxis, 12, 15-16, 59, 60-61, 63, 70-71, 81-82

Series Published by Wilfrid Laurier University Press for the Canadian Corporation for Studies in Religion / Corporation Canadienne des Sciences Religieuses

Editions SR

1. *La langue de Ya'udi : description et classement de l'ancien parler de Zencircli dans le cadre des langues sémitiques du nord-ouest*
   Paul-Eugène Dion, O.P.
   1974 / viii + 511 p. / OUT OF PRINT

2. *The Conception of Punishment in Early Indian Literature*
   Terence P. Day
   1982 / iv + 328 pp.

3. *Traditions in Contact and Change: Selected Proceedings of the XIVth Congress of the International Association for the History of Religions*
   Edited by Peter Slater and Donald Wiebe with Maurice Boutin and Harold Coward
   1983 / x + 758 pp. / OUT OF PRINT

4. *Le messianisme de Louis Riel*
   Gilles Martel
   1984 / xviii + 483 p.

5. *Mythologies and Philosophies of Salvation in the Theistic Traditions of India*
   Klaus K. Klostermaier
   1984 / xvi + 549 pp. / OUT OF PRINT

6. *Averroes' Doctrine of Immortality: A Matter of Controversy*
   Ovey N. Mohammed
   1984 / vi + 202 pp. / OUT OF PRINT

7. *L'étude des religions dans les écoles : l'expérience américaine, anglaise et canadienne*
   Fernand Ouellet
   1985 / xvi + 666 p.

8. *Of God and Maxim Guns: Presbyterianism in Nigeria, 1846-1966*
   Geoffrey Johnston
   1988 / iv + 322 pp.

9. *A Victorian Missionary and Canadian Indian Policy: Cultural Synthesis vs Cultural Replacement*
   David A. Nock
   1988 / x + 194 pp. / OUT OF PRINT

10. *Prometheus Rebound: The Irony of Atheism*
    Joseph C. McLelland
    1988 / xvi + 366 pp.

11. *Competition in Religious Life*
    Jay Newman
    1989 / viii + 237 pp.

12. *The Huguenots and French Opinion, 1685-1787: The Enlightenment Debate on Toleration*
    Geoffrey Adams
    1991 / xiv + 335 pp.

13. *Religion in History: The Word, the Idea, the Reality / La religion dans l'histoire : le mot, l'idée, la réalité*
    Edited by/Sous la direction de Michel Despland and/et Gérard Vallée
    1992 / x + 252 pp.

14. *Sharing Without Reckoning: Imperfect Right and the Norms of Reciprocity*
    Millard Schumaker
    1992 / xiv + 112 pp.

15. *Love and the Soul: Psychological Interpretations of the Eros and Psyche Myth*
    James Gollnick
    1992 / viii + 174 pp.
16. *The Promise of Critical Theology: Essays in Honour of Charles Davis*
    Edited by Marc P. Lalonde
    1995 / xii + 146 pp.
17. *The Five Aggregates: Understanding Theravāda, Psychology and Soteriology*
    Mathieu Boisvert
    1995 / xii + 166 pp.
18. *Mysticism and Vocation*
    James R. Horne
    1995 / 152 pp. est. / FORTHCOMING

Comparative Ethics Series /
Collection d'Éthique Comparée

1. *Muslim Ethics and Modernity: A Comparative Study of the Ethical Thought
   of Sayyid Ahmad Khan and Mawlana Mawdudi*
   Sheila McDonough
   1984 / x + 130 pp. / OUT OF PRINT
2. *Methodist Education in Peru: Social Gospel, Politics, and American
   Ideological and Economic Penetration, 1888-1930*
   Rosa del Carmen Bruno-Jofré
   1988 / xiv + 223 pp.
3. *Prophets, Pastors and Public Choices: Canadian Churches and the
   Mackenzie Valley Pipeline Debate*
   Roger Hutchinson
   1992 / xiv + 142 pp.

Dissertations SR

1. *The Social Setting of the Ministry as Reflected in the Writings
   of Hermas, Clement and Ignatius*
   Harry O. Maier
   1991 / viii + 230 pp. / OUT OF PRINT
2. *Literature as Pulpit: The Christian Social Activism of Nellie L. McClung*
   Randi R. Warne
   1993 / viii + 236 pp.

Studies in Christianity and Judaism /
Études sur le christianisme et le judaïsme

1. *A Study in Anti-Gnostic Polemics: Irenaeus, Hippolytus, and Epiphanius*
   Gérard Vallée
   1981 / xii + 114 pp. / OUT OF PRINT
2. *Anti-Judaism in Early Christianity*
   Vol. 1, *Paul and the Gospels*, edited by Peter Richardson with David Granskou
   1986 / x + 232 pp.
   Vol. 2, *Separation and Polemic*
   Edited by Stephen G. Wilson
   1986 / xii + 185 pp.
3. *Society, the Sacred, and Scripture in Ancient Judaism: A Sociology of Knowledge*
   Jack N. Lightstone
   1988 / xiv + 126 pp.
4. *Law in Religious Communities in the Roman Period: The Debate Over
   Torah and Nomos in Post-Biblical Judaism and Early Christianity*
   Peter Richardson and Stephen Westerholm with A. I. Baumgarten,
   Michael Pettem and Cecilia Wassén
   1991 / x + 164 pp.

5. *Dangerous Food: 1 Corinthians 8-10 in Its Context*
   Peter D. Gooch
   1993 / xviii + 178 pp.
6. *The Rhetoric of the Babylonian Talmud, Its Social Meaning and Context*
   Jack N. Lightstone
   1994 / xiv + 317 pp.

The Study of Religion in Canada /
Sciences Religieuses au Canada

1. *Religious Studies in Alberta: A State-of-the-Art Review*
   Ronald W. Neufeldt
   1983 / xiv + 145 pp.
2. *Les sciences religieuses au Québec depuis 1972*
   Louis Rousseau et Michel Despland
   1988 / 158 p.
3. *Religious Studies in Ontario: A State-of-the-Art Review*
   Harold Remus, William Closson James and Daniel Fraikin
   1992 / xviii + 422 pp.
4. *Religious Studies in Manitoba and Saskatchewan: A State-of-the-Art Review*
   John M. Badertscher, Gordon Harland and Roland E. Miller
   1993 / vi + 166 pp.
5. *The Study of Religion in British Columbia: A State-of-the-Art Review*
   Brian J. Fraser
   1995 / 128 pp. est. / FORTHCOMING

SR Supplements

1. *Footnotes to a Theology: The Karl Barth Colloquium of 1972*
   Edited and Introduced by Martin Rumscheidt
   1974 / viii + 151 pp. / OUT OF PRINT
2. *Martin Heidegger's Philosophy of Religion*
   John R. Williams
   1977 / x + 190 pp. / OUT OF PRINT
3. *Mystics and Scholars: The Calgary Conference on Mysticism 1976*
   Edited by Harold Coward and Terence Penelhum
   1977 / viii + 121 pp. / OUT OF PRINT
4. *God's Intention for Man: Essays in Christian Anthropology*
   William O. Fennell
   1977 / xii + 56 pp. / OUT OF PRINT
5. *"Language" in Indian Philosophy and Religion*
   Edited and Introduced by Harold G. Coward
   1978 / x + 98 pp. / OUT OF PRINT
6. *Beyond Mysticism*
   James R. Horne
   1978 / vi + 158 pp. / OUT OF PRINT
7. *The Religious Dimension of Socrates' Thought*
   James Beckman
   1979 / xii + 276 pp. / OUT OF PRINT
8. *Native Religious Traditions*
   Edited by Earle H. Waugh and K. Dad Prithipaul
   1979 / xii + 244 pp. / OUT OF PRINT
9. *Developments in Buddhist Thought: Canadian Contributions to Buddhist Studies*
   Edited by Roy C. Amore
   1979 / iv + 196 pp.
10. *The Bodhisattva Doctrine in Buddhism*
    Edited and Introduced by Leslie S. Kawamura
    1981 / xxii + 274 pp. / OUT OF PRINT

11. *Political Theology in the Canadian Context*
    Edited by Benjamin G. Smillie
    1982 / xii + 260 pp.
12. *Truth and Compassion: Essays on Judaism and Religion*
    in Memory of Rabbi Dr. Solomon Frank
    Edited by Howard Joseph, Jack N. Lightstone and Michael D. Oppenheim
    1983 / vi + 217 pp.
13. *Craving and Salvation: A Study in Buddhist Soteriology*
    Bruce Matthews
    1983 / xiv + 138 pp. / OUT OF PRINT
14. *The Moral Mystic*
    James R. Horne
    1983 / x + 134 pp.
15. *Ignatian Spirituality in a Secular Age*
    Edited by George P. Schner
    1984 / viii + 128 pp. / OUT OF PRINT
16. *Studies in the Book of Job*
    Edited by Walter E. Aufrecht
    1985 / xii + 76 pp.
17. *Christ and Modernity: Christian Self-Understanding in a Technological Age*
    David J. Hawkin
    1985 / x + 181 pp.
18. *Young Man Shinran: A Reappraisal of Shinran's Life*
    Takamichi Takahatake
    1987 / xvi + 228 pp. / OUT OF PRINT
19. *Modernity and Religion*
    Edited by William Nicholls
    1987 / vi + 191 pp.
20. *The Social Uplifters: Presbyterian Progressives and the*
    Social Gospel in Canada, 1875-1915
    Brian J. Fraser
    1988 / xvi + 212 pp. / OUT OF PRINT

Available from / en vente chez :

WILFRID LAURIER UNIVERSITY PRESS
Waterloo, Ontario, Canada   N2L 3C5